Praise for *Crazy Good Interviewing*

"I work with businesses to help them improve performance and profitability. Businesses look for the right people, and hire those who win in the interview process. If you know someone who is about to graduate, this is a perfect graduation gift. If your adult son or daughter wants to move back home, they need this book, too!"

—Joe Calloway,
author, *Becoming a Category of One*

"Enlightening, engaging, and highly empowering! This book is a MUST READ if you want to know how to GET that job!"

—Monica Wofford,
CSP, CEO, Contagious Companies, Inc.,
author, *Make Difficult People Disappear*

"John is a master presenter and a leading authority on the conduct of the selection interview. His wise counsel will serve you well if you need advice on preparing for and standing out in an interview setting."

—Carol Elam, EdD,
Associate Dean for Admissions
and Institutional Advancement,
University of Kentucky College of Medicine

"This book is a job seeker's bible. If you need a job, you need this book. I plan on anonymously leaving it by the bedside of several family members."

—Molly Cox,
co-author, *Improvise This!*

"I taught John the basics of interviewing while sitting around the dining room table. He'll teach you that and so much more. Be good to yourself—get this book!"

—Mary K. Molidor,
Mom, Grandma, and Grandma the Great

CRAZY GOOD INTERVIEWING

CRAZY GOOD INTER- VIEWING

How Acting a Little Crazy Can Get You the Job

You got the job.

JOHN B. MOLIDOR, PhD

WITH BARBARA PARUS

WILEY

John Wiley & Sons, Inc.

Published by John Wiley & Sons, Inc., Hoboken, New Jersey
Published simultaneously in Canada

For general information on our other products and services or for technical support, please contact our Customer Care Department within the United States at (800) 762-2974, outside the United States at (317) 572-3993 or fax (317) 572-4002.

Wiley publishes in a variety of print and electronic formats and by print-on-demand. Some material included with standard print versions of this book may not be included in e-books or in print-on-demand. If this book refers to media such as a CD or DVD that is not included in the version you purchased, you may download this material at http://booksupport.wiley.com. For more information about Wiley products, visit www.wiley.com.

Library of Congress Cataloging-in-Publication Data:
Molidor, John B., 1951–
  Crazy good interviewing : how acting a little crazy can get you the job / John B. Molidor, PhD, with Barbara Parus.
    ISBN 978-1-118-29514-4 (pbk); ISBN 978-1-118-33184-2 (ebk); ISBN 978-1-118-33405-8 (ebk); ISBN 978-1-118-33516-1 (ebk)
    1. Employement interviewing. 2. Job hunting. 3. Personality. I. Parus, Barbara. II. Title.
    HF5549.5.I6
    650.14′4–dc23

2012006126

Printed in the United States of America.

10 9 8 7 6 5 4 3 2 1

To Our Parents

Otto B. Molidor
One of the great executive recruiters and dads

Mary K. Molidor
One of the great master interviewers and moms

Anthony E. Parus
One of the great multitalented and multilingual dads

Erica J. Parus
One of the world's most beautiful and supportive moms

Contents

Foreword

When I first met John B. Molidor, Ph.D., I fell in love with him. Everyone else does, too.

He's, well, unusual, both as a dean of a college of medicine and as a CEO. He's also unusual because he is a professor of psychiatry and a master presenter. He loves observing people, figuring out what makes them tick, and then teaching us how to use this information.

Along the way, he forgot to grow up. Intentionally. He gets something very few people get: People who make a massive difference take their results seriously and themselves lightly.

He is the epitome of "Let's knock it out of the park . . . and while we're at it, didja hear the one about the rabbi, the priest, and the minister who walked into a bar and asked to interview the bartender?"

He stays light. He just can't help himself. But don't kid yourself. Even as he's yucking it up, he's moving mountains. One huge area of his expertise is how people perceive others and how they make judgments about them— instantly. This has played nicely into his interest in the selection interview and how it works. But, more importantly, he shows us how to use this information to manage this process.

On so many occasions over the years I've known him, I've seen him light up like a light bulb as he explained to me how he, as one of the deans of the medical school, helped his students get the jobs they want. It's a play-by-play about each student . . . what they did to get ready for their interview, how they performed in the interview, and how they put it all together to seal the deal.

Just by looking at him, you know this man is no stuffed shirt academic. Take his teaching uniform, for example: dress slacks topped with a Hawaiian shirt in a colorful floral print. Keep in mind that he lives in Michigan with its frigid winters. But, by no means does his casual attire reflect his attitude: He's a man on a mission. He not only taught thousands of people lessons on how to land a job, he taught them a far more powerful and additional lesson: how to be in the workplace and in life. He hammers home the importance of being authentic and being the best you that you can be.

John wrote *Crazy Good Interviewing* about how to get the job you want, based on his many years of conducting workshops and teaching interview techniques. When the idea for this book was just a seed in his brain, he was searching for the right person to help him germinate his vision. Where would he find such a person?

His keen observational skills, combined with his vast interview experience, led him to Barbara Parus, a writer extraordinaire who has a knack for transforming dry subject matter into fun, reader-friendly prose. The two seemed to be an ideal fit. They are both big-picture people with an irreverent sense of humor. John, who is very methodical and analytical, asked me what it was like working with Barbara, who had interviewed me for a magazine cover story. Happily, I gave her the thumbs up. This set the ball in motion for *Crazy Good Interviewing*.

Knowing how to interview—using the strategies, behaviors, and skills covered in this book—will help you get the job. But it's also your job to be the same person who showed up for the interview and received the job offer.

Do you remember your first day of work? You arrived with your shirt pressed and your shoes shined. You told everyone that you were going to set the world afire and your pent-up energy was ready to explode. In a perfect world, you were ready to make a difference as a valued member of the team, produce attention-grabbing results, and start climbing the job ladder.

But what if the opposite happened? Two weeks went by and you discovered the work environment wasn't exactly ideal and you worked with a bunch of, well, dweebs—whiners, gossips, and drama queens—all moving relentlessly toward mediocrity! You wondered, "How did this happen?"

You probably forgot that the interview is a two-way process. You were so focused on getting the employer to like you that you didn't pay attention to a bigger question: Do you like them?

If you're a Gen Yer, you might jump ship, only to find that it happens again, and again, and again. There is no perfect workplace.

During my years of speaking, I've asked hundreds of thousands of people if they can relate to that scenario. Wherever I go, without exception, heads nod almost universally. You will need to step up your game of leadership to make your job perfect.

And that is when you get to be the person John shows you how to be in the interview—the woman or man who is filled with passion to make a difference through your work and a leader in helping the people around you get it. You use your interpersonal skills, body language, and powers of persuasion to rally the troops, motivate co-workers, and make meaningful contributions as part of the team.

So, go get that job. Then, if it falls short of your ideal, use your power of three and your unique value proposition to turn it into the job you interviewed for. What if instead of dragging yourself to work each week, you said, "Thank God It's Monday!" and couldn't wait to go to play? Now, that sounds like a good job to me . . . a crazy good job!

Rock on!

Roxanne Emmerich,
author of *Thank God It's Monday!: How to*
Create the Workplace You and Your Customers Love

Acknowledgments

From John B. Molidor, Ph.D.

Big acknowledgments go to:

My current and former medical students, *who taught me about what they were encountering on the interview trail and what they needed to know to nail the interview and get the job.*

My current and former pre-medical and pre-professional students, *who taught me about the importance (and anxiety) of high-stakes interviewing.*

My fellow admissions officers, deans, directors, and program directors (from medicine, business, dentistry, law, and other corporate associations and industries), *who showed me how they interviewed and selected their best and brightest.*

My friends from both of my NSA worlds: from the National Speakers Association (especially Joe Calloway, Roxanne Emmerich, Marilynn Semonick, C. Leslie Charles, Chris Clarke-Epstein, Terry Paulson, Mark Sanborn, Phil Van Hooser, Lou Heckler, Terry Brock, Ian Percy, Janita Cooper, Ed Scannell, Ed Gerety, and Kevin O'Connor) and from the National Safety Associates (especially Jay Martin, Randy Matthews and Ron Watkins), *who have influenced me, encouraged me, and celebrated with me along this journey.*

My colleagues from Michigan State University's College of Human Medicine and Michigan State University's Flint Area Medical Education, *who can say they knew me when and who have supported me over the years in my various roles as a faculty member, dean, and CEO.*

My friends and classmates from the College of St. Thomas (now the University of St. Thomas) and Michigan State University, *who first saw me as a young pup as I started on this adventure toward cognitive psychology and how people make decisions about other people and how this affects their lives.*

My old friend, Paul Elliott, Ph.D. (Florida State University), *who first suggested that as a freshly minted faculty member and dean, I carefully pick key areas of expertise to explore as part of my life's work.* Who knew that one of them would be interviewing and that it would come full circle to this book?

My family (especially my mom and dad and all of my siblings—Steve, Kathy, Dan, Mary Clare, Lisa, Jim, Kevin, Larry, and Tom—as well as their spouses and partners, my nieces and nephews, and my great nieces and nephews), *who have shown me the incredible blessing and value of having such a loving and supportive family.*

A special thanks to my Aunt Oopie (Sister Christian Molidor, R.S.M.), *who has always believed I had a book (or two or three or more) in me and who has encouraged me along the way to get it down on paper (or on the computer) and get it out to the world.*

A special thanks to my collaborator, Barbara Parus, *who was a joy to work with and made this book become a reality with her extraordinary research skills and writing talent, razor-sharp wit, and dedication to seeing this project through to fruition. She made concepts and ideas come alive through humor, words, and stories.*

A huge and loving thanks to my son, Christopher D. Molidor, *who has endured years of being interviewed by me and whose good nature and spirit make me proud every day.*

A big special, heartfelt and loving thanks to Pamela R. Benitez, M.D., *who has stood by me throughout this process and who has taught me to pay particular attention to the feeling aspect of all things that are good in life.*

To all of you, a big thank you.

From Barbara Parus

Big acknowledgments go to:

My loving parents, Anthony E. and Erica J. Parus, *who have always believed in my abilities and think I am one smart cookie.*

My son, Daniel Steven Max, *who is my inspiration and has encouraged me to reach for the stars.*

My sister, Patricia Parus Horwitz, *who patiently listened to me while I worked on this book for more than a year.*

Last, but not least, John B. Molidor, Ph.D., *who used his "crazy good" interviewing skills to recognize my talent and work ethic, and determined that we would make a crazy good book duo.*

To all of you, many thanks!

From John and Barbara

Special thanks to:

Dan Ambrosio and Tiffany Colón, at John Wiley & Sons, who guided us through the process of birthing a book.

Design and marketing team at Wiley & Sons, *who made us look crazy good on the outside.*

Bill Van Nimwegen of Vanim Design, *who created the illustrations in* Crazy Good Interviewing *to make us look crazy good on the inside.*

And finally, all of our readers and job seekers, *who are out there doing what has to be done to get the job and then some.*

1 | Job Hunting in a Crazy Economy

Could you stand up and sing in a Karaoke bar? In front of complete strangers? Without any practice? With little or no lead time?

If your vocal talent is similar to Tony Bennett, Michael Bublé, Christina Aguilera, Seal, or Lady Gaga, you would undoubtedly enjoy doing this, even basking in the afterglow of audience applause and whistles from your newfound fans chanting "Encore!"

If your voice is mediocre at best, or if you are sorely out of practice, you know what it feels like to sing your heart out trying to imitate your favorite performer only to be met with laughter, groans, and rude remarks such as: "Next," "Get out of here," or "Don't give up your day job!"

Translation: If you don't know what you're doing (even if your intentions are good), you're going to be in trouble. Moreover, if you quit your regular paying job to become a singer, you will starve.

This type of negative reaction can be disheartening at best.

In today's tough economy, I don't know many people who are contemplating quitting a secure, well-paying job to become a singer or turn their other passions or hobbies into an income-generating business. In

1

fact, most people consider themselves lucky if they have a job at all. For many people who are unemployed, though, their full-time job is looking for a job.

Job Market Overview

By definition, persons are classified as unemployed if they do not have a job, have been actively looking for work for the past four weeks, and are currently available for work. With unemployment hovering around 9 percent at the end of 2011, according to the U.S. Bureau of Labor Statistics (BLS), it's no wonder many people are discouraged at their prospects of finding employment, especially in their chosen fields. Add in those who have stopped hunting for jobs, and the numbers soar to 11 percent nationwide.

Everyone is familiar with tales of the Great Depression, which sparked the stock market crash and forced millions of people into the unemployment line. But did you know that the Great Recession, launched in December 2007, has put more people out of work for longer periods of time since the Great Depression? The fact is 6.4 million people have been jobless for at least six months, and 1.4 million have been unemployed for two years or longer.

The country is experiencing the greatest recession since the Great Depression with 9.2 percent unemployment reported in October 2011. Unemployment rates rose in 28 states and Washington, D.C., according to the BLS. Nevada had the highest unemployment rate for the 18th straight month (13.4 percent), followed by California (11.7 percent) and Michigan (10.6 percent).

If these statistics don't motivate you to hone your interviewing skills, then nothing will. It's time to consider your options if you're not independently wealthy or the holder of a winning lottery ticket.

If you cannot pack up and move to North Dakota, which boasts the nation's lowest unemployment rate of only 3.5 percent, Nebraska (4.2 percent), South Dakota (4.5 percent), or New Hampshire (5.3 percent), then you must have a winning job interview strategy in place. Table 1.1 lists unemployment rates by state.

Is there an end in sight to this bleak employment picture? Well, maybe. The non-partisan Congressional Budget Office (CBO) projected

Table 1.1　United States Unemployment Rates by State

Rank	Modified November 22, 2011 State	Rate
1	North Dakota	3.5
2	Nebraska	4.2
3	South Dakota	4.5
4	New Hampshire	5.3
5	Vermont	5.6
6	Wyoming	5.7
7	Iowa	6.0
8	Oklahoma	6.1
9	Minnesota	6.4
9	Virginia	6.4
11	Hawaii	6.5
12	New Mexico	6.6
13	Kansas	6.7
14	Louisiana	7.0
14	Utah	7.0
16	Maryland	7.2
17	Maine	7.3
17	Massachusetts	7.3
19	Alaska	7.4
20	Montana	7.6
21	Wisconsin	7.7
22	New York	7.9
24	Pennsylvania	8.1
25	Colorado	8.1
26	Arkansas	8.2
26	West Virginia	8.2
28	Texas	8.4
29	Missouri	8.5
30	Connecticut	8.7
31	Idaho	8.8
32	Ohio	9.0
32	Indiana	9.0
32	Washington	9.0

(Continued)

Table 1.1 (*Continued*)

Rank	Modified November 22, 2011 State	Rate
32	Arizona	9.0
36	New Jersey	9.1
37	Alabama	9.3
38	Oregon	9.5
39	Kentucky	9.6
39	Tennessee	9.6
41	Illinois	10.1
42	Georgia	10.2
43	Florida	10.3
44	North Carolina	10.4
44	Rhode Island	10.4
46	Mississippi	10.5
47	South Carolina	10.6
47	Michigan	10.6
49	District of Columbia	11.0
50	California	11.7
51	Nevada	13.4

that unemployment will decrease to 8 percent in 2012, but don't count on it dropping to a more normal 5.3 percent until 2016.

But no matter where you live in the United States, nobody's escaping today's tough economy. Seasoned workers and newbies alike are nervous about their jobs, even in states where the unemployment rate is relatively low compared to the rest of the nation.

Every day, multibillion-dollar companies and small privately owned businesses alike are handing out pink slips. Whether you are working for a conglomerate or a family-owned business, it does not matter. Everyone's job is at stake. People are holding onto the jobs they have even if they feel dissatisfied, unappreciated, or unfulfilled in their careers.

It's scary to search for a job in a tough market. The worse the economy is, the harder it is to get and keep a good job. With a bad economy and no credentials, sometimes it feels almost futile to search when jobs are in such short supply.

Yet hiring across the country has not come to a complete halt. Jobs exist, but fewer openings and more competition mean they're not all that easy to come by. If you're looking for your first job, or if you're out of work and looking, your task is to get into extreme job search mode to land a job interview, and then do everything in your power to shine during the interview. This is your time to stand up and sing, even if you don't sound like Tony, Michael, Christina, Seal, or Gaga.

Why Is the Interview So Important?

The interview allows someone (typically the interviewer or company) to gather information about you, which would be difficult or impossible to obtain by any other means. The interview provides your reviewer with information crucial in evaluating your potential and fit for the job. For example, a job candidate who is vying for the slot as a communications director or a corporate spokesperson must have top-notch verbal skills, sales managers must have a proven track record, and hair stylists must have an existing and satisfied clientele. The interview is usually the deciding factor in determining whether you get the job.

Many interviewers use a list of established questions while others may develop their own questions, discussion areas, and problem-solving behaviors. Even though there is no set procedure for beginning an interview, the opening minutes are critical to your success. This is where having a strategy in place, practicing, and being ready to perform will impact how you start your interview.

Bookstores and the Internet are inundated with resources and how-to guides that list countless creative ways to hunt for a job and land an interview. Everyone is networking and using social media tools like Facebook and LinkedIn to establish connections and build relationships that will lead to job interviews.

The marketplace, however, has limited sources that provide job hunters with a bona fide step-by-step program for preparing for the interview—a process that coaches them on the proper behaviors to exhibit to help them stand out in a sea of job candidates—especially one that is based on science and research.

When you are lucky enough to snag an interview, you need a tried-and-true strategy you can implement immediately and that makes you rise to the top like the proverbial cream of the crop, nail the interview, and get the job offer.

An effective job interview strategy can be your hidden ace in the hole for getting a job offer, whether you are seeking your first job out of school, you were recently laid off, you are seeking a key position, you are trying to get into a professional school, or you are ready to make a career change.

With intense competition for jobs, many candidates are attempting more creative approaches to get noticed. A little ingenuity may help get you noticed. You do not, however, need to send a singing telegram, a bouquet of balloons, or a tin filled with homemade cookies to a prospective employer's office to attract attention. Just be sure you spend as much time preparing for the interview as you do landing the meeting.

So, what is the silver bullet for learning to put your best foot forward during the interview, effectively engaging the interviewer, and ultimately landing the job?

Enter "Crazy Good Interviewing." No, this term does not imply that you act like a crazed lunatic. Crazy good means excellent or out of the ordinary. The word interview refers to a formal meeting (typically in-person although phone and Skype are being used more often these days), especially one arranged for assessing an applicant's qualifications. You will learn the skills and behaviors to have an excellent formal meeting.

In essence, crazy good interviewing is all about applying a variety of mental strategies and positive verbal and non-verbal communication skills to the interview process to ensure the best possible outcome. Let me, though, set things straight from the onset. There is no one right way to interview. Many ways are successful. The key is using an underlying process and model.

Successful crazy good interviewing depends on creating situations in which information, ideas, values, and feelings can be exchanged freely, easily, clearly, and directly. Job applicants pray for this best-case scenario.

Unfortunately, not all interviews are smooth sailing. What would you do, for example, if you're cruising along in the interview, and all of a sudden, the interaction between you and the interviewer stalls and starts going downhill? What happens when you're ready to tell your story, and the interviewer does not let you get a word in edgewise?

By learning how to interview in a crazy good way, you will recover quickly from these and any other stumbling blocks or hurdles that arise.

What Makes Me an Expert?

I have provided hundreds of training programs for professional schools ranging from medical schools to graduate medical education residency programs, for associations ranging from law to executive MBA programs, and for organizations ranging from small businesses to hospitals.

I have taught thousands of individuals how to design an effective selection interview. In other words, I have trained these individuals to become insightful, structured, and decisive interviewers. I, too, have interviewed hundreds of individuals for various positions over the years.

All this was fine and good until my students and colleagues asked me, or rather, demanded that I address the flip side of interviewing, namely, how they could master the art of being interviewed, which is at the heart of crazy good interviewing. From this request, I developed a new training workshop, which morphed and evolved into a high-stakes crazy good interviewing model called ACT Out. ACT is an acronym for:

- **A**ssess: How to review your strengths and qualifications as they pertain to the position.
- **C**ommunicate: How to use verbal and non-verbal skills to engage the interviewer(s).
- **T**hank: How to follow up after the interview, thank, and stay connected with your interviewer(s).

The ACT Out model provides individuals with a detailed blueprint outlining how to approach the interview, how to execute an effective interview exchange, and how to follow up after the interview. The model is based on years of observing the successes and pitfalls of individual interviewees, huge doses of common sense, and psychological research into the areas of communication, neuroscience, emotional intelligence, and personality types.

This psychological research plays a large part in the crazy good portion of the meeting; the face-to-face encounter refers to the interviewing part as described in the title of this book.

The skills needed to obtain a prized position, whether you are applying for a job (e.g., management track, senior level, or CEO) or applying to get into a professional program (e.g., medical colleges, business schools, or residency programs), are basically the same:

- Create rapport quickly.
- Communicate clearly, directly, and effectively.
- Observe and understand what is going on within the interview room.
- Answer all questions thoughtfully and thoroughly.
- Relate answers to the position at hand.
- Show a crazy good fit between you and the job.

In high-stakes positions and professional school situations, you will typically encounter a competitive environment because more candidates exist than positions. In today's economy, this seems to be the case for jobs.

The interview can provoke anxiety because it is tough being viewed under the microscope as you seek a position or wish to move up to the next level. The interview can be a wild process, so it helps sometimes if you are a little crazy. Not crazy in a paranoid-schizophrenic way. Not crazy in an obsessive-compulsive way. Not crazy in a loud, obnoxious, or inappropriate way. But crazy in a good way, such as exhibiting creative, thoughtful, good common sense behaviors that seem to have fallen by the wayside.

This book will discuss the behaviors, strategies, and communication skills that applicants should exhibit during an interview. As with everything in life, knowing what not to do will help.

This book will introduce the *Psychotron*, which is a measurement tool to gauge crazy good and crazy bad behaviors, strategies, and responses. There will be numerous scenarios sprinkled throughout the chapters in which you will be asked to step into the shoes of the interviewer and rate the behaviors of job candidates using the Psychotron.

Throughout the book, key insights will be highlighted under "The Doctor Is In . . ." signage. I will provide spot-on advice, observations, and witticisms to ensure a crazy good interview learning experience.

The Doctor Is In . . .

"It's critical to hone your interview skills in today's tough and competitive job market. Let me show you how!"

2 | Go Crazy—In a Good Way

If you are new to job hunting, you are probably wondering where you can find reliable information about how to act on job interviews. If you are not new to job hunting, you probably have picked up some bad interview habits along the way, or you are reading some outdated information on interview techniques that has been collecting dust on your bookshelf. You need an interview strategy for today's job marketplace. Times have changed, and you need a competitive edge. Enter crazy good interviewing.

Crazy good interviewing is all about knowing what you should do and not do before, during, and after the interview. It's about getting psyched up—not acting crazy—so you can shine.

The interviewer will take the whole package into consideration during the interview. Your attire, mannerisms, voice inflection, facial expressions, hand gestures, and body language will be scrutinized, along with your answers, and the skills and work experience you bring to the position.

Will your interviewer give you high marks in the same way that audiences applaud seasoned pros like Tony Bennett, Michael Bublé, Christina

Aguilera, Seal, and Lady Gaga? Or will your performance bomb from lack of preparation?

First, it is important to understand how your behaviors impact your interview ratings.

How Do You Rate?

The interviewing process often includes the use of rating scales that interviewers use to evaluate the quality of the interview and lead to some kind of recommendation of the candidate for the job in question. Ratings generally evaluate one or more of the following:

- Responses to individual questions.
- Job-related competencies that may or may not be linked to individual questions posed during the interview.
- The overall interview experience.

So, how do you determine what behaviors are acceptable or unacceptable in the crazy good interviewing process when you are responding to all of the interviewer's questions?

Introducing the "Psychotron"

Throughout this book, a measurement tool called a Psychotron will rate behaviors on a scale of "crazy bad" to "crazy good." The Psychotron is based loosely on the National Superconducting Cyclotron Laboratory (NSCL) at Michigan State University (MSU), a world leader in nuclear science education and rare isotope research. More than 700 scientists from the United States and abroad have come to the NSCL, which is recognized for its nuclear physics research and innovations in accelerator design.

I am on the faculty at MSU, so let me brag and say that *U.S. News and World Report* ranks the MSU Nuclear Physics Program as number one in the nation. The NSCL at MSU operates two superconducting cyclotrons: the K500, which was the world's first cyclotron to use superconducting magnets, and the K1200, which is the highest-energy continuous beam accelerator in the nation. Using these and other related devices, scientists have learned more about the origins of the elements in the cosmos.

With that said, the cyclotron and the Psychotron have similarities other than the two terms sounding alike. The cyclotron accelerates particles and can smash these particles at high speeds into each other to create a reaction. This is similar to the interview process in which two people come together, typically at high speeds, with the goal of achieving some type of reaction, hopefully, a positive one. But not all interviews result in a reaction. If the interview stalls, the atoms (and people) do not create a reaction. Nothing happens. It's like being stuck in *The Twilight Zone* in the longest interview on earth with no exit. There's no engagement, no energy, no give-and-take, and no job offer.

How Does the Psychotron Work?

The Psychotron looks like a heat gauge, which registers the temperature ranging from cold (on the far left) to boiling hot (on the far right). Likewise, the Psychotron measures behaviors from crazy bad (cold on the far left) to crazy good (hot on the far right). The farther the arrow is to the left, the more crazy bad the behavior is. The farther the arrow is to the right, the more crazy good it is. Think of crazy good as being hot stuff.

Rate the Behavior

But the picture is not all black or white. Varying shades of gray craziness lie in between the two extremes. Many behaviors will be borderline, with the arrow pointing smack dab in the middle. In those cases, it is up to the interviewer to judge and decide.

Degrees of Craziness
- Crazy good: Candidate exhibits desirable positive behaviors.
- Slightly sane: There's hope for this candidate.

- Borderline: This behavior is the interviewer's judgment call.
- Slightly insane: Candidate is probably not dangerous, but beware.
- Crazy bad: Certifiably insane; get the straitjacket.

What's Crazy Bad Behavior?

A common complaint among many interviewers, especially older ones, hiring agents, and human resources professionals today is that younger job applicants—namely, those who fall under the Generation X and Generation Y labels—arrive completely unprepared or, worse yet, have a large sense of entitlement.

Though confidence is never a bad thing, you should not show up with the wrong attitude. Any negative behavior can be construed as crazy bad and jeopardize your chances of being viewed as a viable candidate and being considered for the job in question.

What constitutes crazy bad behavior? We are not talking about people who are certifiably insane or ready to be institutionalized even though some candidates may fit the description. Their behaviors simply exhibit a lack of common sense and propriety. Here are some strange, but true, examples. How would you rate each of them on the Psychotron?

Rate the Behavior

- Wearing a baseball cap backward, unless applying for the job of umpire.
  Interviewer thinks, "You're out."
- Checking your cell phone for voice mails and text messages.
  Interviewer thinks, "Is this interview cramping your social life?"

- Asking how many young good-looking chicks or dudes work there.
  Interviewer thinks, "Is this job your answer to Match.com?"
- Asking the interviewer out on a date.
  Interviewer thinks, "You've gotta be kidding me."
- Calling your interviewer Bob or Nancy, instead of Mr. Johnson or Ms. Green.
  Interviewer thinks, "Try again, pal."
- Calling your interviewer Mr. Johnson, when his name is Mr. Jones.
  Interviewer thinks, "Do you have short-term memory loss?"
- Discussing salary, vacation, and other benefits before an offer is extended.
  Interviewee says, "I'll need time off to get my hoo-hoo pierced."
  Interviewer thinks, "Ouch."
- Laughing incessantly or uncontrollably.
  Interviewer thinks, "Dial it down, Nutcase."
- Inquiring about the company's drug testing policy.
  Interviewee says, "How much notice do you give employees?"
  Interviewer thinks, "You just flunked that test."
- Recommending that the interviewer should not do a background check on you.
  Interviewee says, "I wouldn't make the call if I were you."
  Interviewer thinks, "That sounds like a threat."
- Bad-mouthing your former employer or blaming a co-worker for your failures at your last job.
  Interviewee says, "My supervisor was always picking on me."
  Interviewer thinks, "Shut up, you big baby."
- Being overly concerned about the company's position on terminations.
  Interviewee says, "Do you ever press charges?"
  Interviewer thinks, "I might have to call security."
- Dropping the "F" bomb and other swear words.
  Interviewee says, "Oh, shit."
  Interviewer thinks, "This guy just f----d up his chances."
- Lighting up a cigarette or chewing tobacco.
  Interviewee says, "Light me."
  Interviewer thinks, "Can't he read the 'No Smoking' sign?" (cough)
- Yawning.
  Interviewee says, "Yaaaaaaaawn." (Translation: "I'm bored.")
  Interviewer thinks, "Next."

- Uttering monosyllabic responses to the interviewer's open-ended questions.

  Interviewer, "Do you prefer being in a leadership role or working behind the scenes?"

  Interviewee, "Yes."

- Not providing thoughtful responses to the interviewer's questions.

  Interviewer, "What person would you most like to meet, living or dead?"

  Interviewee, "The living one."

- Reeking of alcohol.

  Interviewee burps.

  Interviewer thinks, "It's 5 o'clock somewhere."

- Acknowledging that you slacked on your last job.

  Interviewer, "What was your greatest accomplishment at your last job?"

  Interviewee, "Writing a romance novel."

  Interviewer, "No, I mean something you did while at work."

  Interviewee, "I wrote it at work."

- Exhibiting multiple personality disorder and introducing the "others."

  Interviewee asks, "Would you like to talk to Karen now? She's the friendly one."

  Interviewer thinks, "I think I hear *Twilight Zone* music playing."

- Constant sniffing.

  Interviewer thinks, "Coke. It's the real thing."

The Doctor Is In . . .

"If you are offered coffee, politely refuse. It could spill and create a distraction during the interview. Coffee relaxes the sphincter and you might need to make a mad dash for the restroom."

What's Crazy Good Behavior?

Crazy good behaviors are not over the top. Nowadays, being normal is enough to get a job in some cases, especially when the other candidates bombed in their interviews and exhibited some of the unacceptable behaviors listed above. For high-stakes positions, being prepared and thinking creatively can help you showcase your experience and qualifications in the best light and separate you from other well-qualified candidates.

Rate the Behavior

Here are some examples of common sense, crazy good behaviors. How would you rate each action on the Psychotron?

- Visit the company website before your interview to bone up on the organization.
- Prepare thoughtful questions to ask the interviewer.
- Wear attire that reflects your professionalism yet sets you apart from other candidates; for example, wear a tasteful, colorful tie for men, a chic scarf for women.
- Arrive 20 minutes early and be friendly and courteous to the person sitting at the reception desk.
- Greet the interviewer with a smile and a firm handshake.
- Know the top three traits you bring to the job and relate examples of each.
- Tell a real-life story that captures, personifies, and exemplifies the qualities and characteristics you will bring to the job.
- Use gestures that illustrate the key points you are making.
- Use self-effacing humor to describe lessons learned.
- Put together a DVD that highlights your abilities.
- Create a presentation on your iPad to show the interviewer what you would bring to the job.
- Compile a CD of songs that inspire you and explain why they motivate you.

- Showcase your skills and talents that pertain to the job; for example, bring samples of your award-winning published articles for a job that requires a lot of writing, or illustrations for a graphic design position.
- Recount your experience helping children at an orphanage in Guatemala.
- Describe your comeback after being seriously injured in a car accident.
- Identify lessons learned about teamwork as a crewmember in the Chicago Yacht Club race across Lake Michigan to Mackinac Island.
- Thank the interviewer for his/her time and follow up with a handwritten note.

The Doctor Is In . . .

"Give the interviewer a firm handshake. Your hand should never feel like a dead fish. Limp hand = limp impression."

Rate the Behavior

Using the Psychotron, how would you rate the behaviors of the job candidates in the following interviews on a scale from crazy bad to crazy good?

Three's a Charm

A job candidate, who was scheduled for a 9 a.m. interview for a sales position, was instructed to bring two forms of identification and three references. At 8:45 a.m., four women walked into the office. The interviewee informed the receptionist that she was scheduled for a 9 a.m. interview with Dr. Molidor. When asked who her three companions were, she said, "They are my references."

Is this crazy bad behavior because the interviewee misunderstood the directive? Is it crazy good behavior because anyone who can persuade three people to accompany her to a morning interview must be a top-notch salesperson?

Nano Nano

When the job candidate entered the room, the interviewer invited him to have a seat. The candidate walked over to the chair, bent forward, and placed his head in the seat.

Is this crazy bad behavior because the interviewee must have been crazy? Is it crazy good behavior because it was a young actor named Robin Williams who was auditioning for the role of a space alien named Mork from Ork on *Happy Days* in 1974? When producer Gary Marshall asked him to sit down, Williams sat on his head. Marshall hired him because he was the only alien who auditioned for the part. The producers were so pleased with Williams' ad libbing that he did not have to stick to the scripts when *Mork & Mindy* was launched in 1978.

The Great Escape

When I asked the candidate how she came to apply for the job, she replied: "It was pouring rain and the wind raged around us. I overheard one of the men say, 'Are you crazy? We can't make it in this weather. It's the monsoon season. We're already drenched like rats and freezing. And if we get caught, the men will be killed and the women and children tortured and maimed for sure.'

"The other man replied, 'We have no choice. There is no turning back. We must go.' Suddenly, a pair of hands lifted me onto a boat. Thus, at the age of six, I began my journey from Vietnam to the United States. I arrived not knowing a single word of English.

"So, if you are looking for someone who will bring determination, tenaciousness, and a sense of responsibility to this position, I know I am that person."

Did the applicant exhibit crazy bad behavior because she chose to regale me with a heart-wrenching tale of her escape from Vietnam rather than focus on the position itself, or is it crazy good behavior because she painted a picture that captured the positive characteristics she developed as a result of her adversity?

3

First Impressions Are Lasting Impressions

Take five. Or seven. Or 30. No, I'm not talking about putting down this ground-breaking book to take a rest break, fix a sandwich, or watch Dr. Phil. I'm referring to the number of seconds it takes for someone to size you up on a first meeting—and make a fairly accurate assessment—according to numerous research studies.

People can absorb an enormous amount of visual information when they encounter other people for the first time. This was a lifesaving capability in earlier times when people needed to protect themselves from neighboring tribes. In the deep, primitive recesses of the brain, they developed a way to quickly determine friend or foe before wielding their prehistoric clubs. Should you invite Cro-Magnon Man back to the cave for a wooly mammoth burger or bash him over the head with a club? Determining perceived affinity or distrust of an individual within seconds was critical. Simply put: Eat or be eaten.

First impressions are surprisingly accurate and can make or break your job interview, your Karaoke performance, or even a first date. Various research studies by social psychologists have found that strangers will form an opinion of you within 2 to 30 seconds of meeting you. Although you might not like someone sizing you up before interviewing you, it is human nature. So, use this information to your benefit if you want to be crazy good before the interviewing process even begins.

In fact, 10—count 'em, 10—psychological judgments are made during a first impression, according to William Thourby in his book, *You Are What You Wear*, including success level, economic status, integrity, education level, social position, level of sophistication, economic heritage, social heritage, educational heritage, and moral character. So much information is absorbed in so little time.

We immediately judge people based on their outward appearance. Are they attractive in terms of personal grooming, and are they wearing sharp, contemporary, appropriate clothing? Do their body language and facial expressions convey confidence? Are they friendly? Are they likeable? Would we want to associate with them?

Look at the Research

Many well-known academic research studies support the accuracy of first impressions. In 1993, Nalini Ambady and Robert Rosenthal of the Harvard Department of Psychology demonstrated that it takes only a few seconds to make a deep and lasting first impression. They recorded 2-, 6-, and 10-second video clips of individual professors, and then asked a group of students to watch the clips and evaluate each professor.

Ambady and Rosenthal compared the evaluations of the students who watched these clips with the evaluations of people who had substantial interactions with those professors. The similarities were amazing. They found that the ratings of complete strangers, based on very thin and short slices of behavior, from 2 to 10 seconds long, accurately predicted the evaluations of people who had interacted regularly with the professors.

Robert Cialdini, Ph.D., of the University of Arizona and author of the best-selling book, *Influence: The Psychology of Persuasion* (first published in 1984), showed that people use shortcuts when judging people. The most common shortcut is looking good equals good. Translation: If you look good, you must be good.

Looking good gets you some breaks in life. Cialdini found in mock jury trials that if you are being sued, you will pay much less to the person who sues you if you look good. Conversely, if you are the one who is suing and you don't look good, the judge will award you less money. What's the lesson? Look good.

Exceptions to the Rule

Once the first impression is formed, it's very difficult to reverse, but it's not entirely impossible. Take Scottish singer Susan Boyle's legendary audition on the TV show, *Britain's Got Talent*, in April 2009. When frumpy Boyle marched on stage with her frizzy, shapeless hair and plain gold-colored dress, the audience and judges had no idea what they were about to experience. Judge Simon Cowell inquired about Boyle's age, to which she placed her hands on her undulating hips and responded, "I'm 47, and that's just one side of me." (Note: Susan's unpolished appearance and hip-swinging movements are examples of crazy bad behavior.)

Snickering audience members rolled their eyes, preparing for a total train wreck. But their jaws dropped instantly when Susan opened her mouth and belted out *I Dreamed a Dream* from *Les Misérables*. At the end of the song, judge Piers Morgan remarked, "Without a doubt, that's the biggest surprise I've had in three years on the show." Boyle's performance was viewed some 300 million times on YouTube, and she became a global singing sensation within days.

The adage "You can't judge a book by its cover" rings true in the case of Landau Eugene Murphy, Jr., a 36-year-old car washer from Logan, West Virginia. Murphy's audition for TV's *America's Got Talent* aired June 22, 2011. Before Murphy broke into song, viewers watched a video clip of him washing cars at an auto dealership. As he soaped up a car with a big sponge, he joked that he didn't want to see any more BF Goodrich tires because he had it up to here with bubbles, motioning to his neck. "It's time to go somewhere and do something else," he said.

Murphy, a mild-mannered African-American male wearing baggy jeans and flowing dreadlocks, was reprimanded by Piers Morgan for chewing gum at his on-stage audition in front of the panel of four judges and a packed auditorium. (Note: Under these circumstances, chewing gum is a crazy bad behavior.) Without breaking eye contact, Murphy heeded Morgan's advice and, with a little smirk on his face, removed the gum from his mouth and stuffed it into his pants pocket.

The judges were unimpressed with Murphy's appearance and did not expect much from him in the way of talent. Then, Landau wowed the full house by nailing a perfect-pitch rendition of Frank Sinatra's *I've Got You Under My Skin*. The surprised judges unanimously voted Murphy—who "never auditioned for anything or anyone" in his life—through to the second round of auditions in Las Vegas.

After Murphy's performance, comedian Howie Mandel, one of the judges on the panel, said, "The performance was such a surprise . . . the music . . . compared to the look," a statement that prompted uproarious laughter from the audience. Murphy said that's precisely why he selected the Sinatra tune. Murphy was an exception to the rule. He knew he was perceived in a certain way, and he deliberately selected a Rat Pack song that did not fit his stereotype, so he would completely shock the judges and audience.

Murphy's audition video became an Internet sensation, and each week fans continued to watch him on TV and view videos of his performances as he kept advancing in the competition. On September 15, 2011, Murphy was crowned as the winner of *America's Got Talent*, and he received a $1 million prize and a Las Vegas headlining contract. The next day, he stopped by *Good Day LA*, a weekday news-talk show on FOX, and told viewers that he planned to use the money to purchase health insurance and start college funds for his three children, further cementing his amiable, down-to-earth charm in the hearts of his fans nationwide.

When you interview for a job, you can also apply the "exception to the rule" example by showing another side of yourself that contrasts with people's perception of you. If you are a formal, academic type, you can show your humorous, playful, or less formal side. The distinct contrast is an example of crazy good behavior. I am a good example of this tactic. My colorful Hawaiian-print shirts, which I wear when presenting throughout the year—in sweltering hot summers and frigid cold winters—have become my signature look. This attire is in sharp contrast with my serious academic role at Michigan State University (MSU), in which most people expect me to wear more conservative clothing.

Although Susan Boyle and Landau Eugene Murphy, Jr., are exceptions to the rule in the entertainment world, there are many other everyday examples that illustrate this point.

Look around you. Have you have noticed a shy, nervous-looking individual who can get up in front of a large audience, speak from the heart, and wow everyone in the room? Or the introvert who rarely chimes in until his or her values are being overridden and then stands tall and rallies the organization to do what is right? Although the adage "you can't judge a book by its cover" generally holds true, there are always exceptions.

The Rating Game

If you were the interviewer, how would you rate the following candidates on the Psychotron, who are applying for a position at your company? Some of these examples are strange but true.

- A woman wearing a blue blazer and matching skirt, conservative shoes, simple jewelry, and toting a sleek leather portfolio of work samples, arrived late for the interview and apologized for being stuck in a traffic jam.
- A young man wearing a bright blue Mohawk, a soul patch, and sporting a pierced tongue and long purple fingernails, jokingly told the interviewer not to "bust his chops."
- A clean-shaven man with a tidy haircut showed up 20 minutes early for his interview, wearing a pressed golf shirt, khaki pants, and leather loafers. He waited patiently in the reception area until the interviewer appeared. Then he stood, smiled, introduced himself, and gave the interviewer a firm handshake.
- A young woman wearing heavy make-up, a low-cut red sweater (overflowing with cleavage), a short skirt, stiletto heels, and lots of chunky jewelry was informed that the interviewer was running behind schedule. The receptionist asked if she'd like coffee and donuts while waiting. She responded, "Yeah. *Them* are good."
- An impeccably groomed man wearing a navy blue suit, dress shirt, a red "power" tie, and polished shoes arrived early and conducted business on his cell phone while waiting for his interview appointment.
- A sharply dressed female candidate wondered aloud to staff members why anyone would want to take a job here.

- A male applicant, who answered his cell phone during the interview, told the person on the other end that he couldn't talk right now because he was in an interview, and then he proceeded to talk anyway (as he got up from his chair and paced around the interviewer's office).
- A woman, who had perused the company's website, commented that she could bring some expertise to the company's newest contract negotiation, based on her past job experience.
- A male candidate indicated that he needed to speak with his mother to make sure he had mentioned all of his qualifications.
- A female applicant, who arrived one day early for her interview because she was so eager, asked if she could help out since she was there anyway.

Rate the Behavior

Stereotypes? Yes, but there's something to be said for stereotypes. The term means a commonly held notion or opinion of a group of people based on an oversimplification of observed behavior. A job candidate who dresses professionally and exudes confidence is making a serious effort to make a favorable impression. In contrast, candidates in casual attire are often viewed as possessing a lax attitude about work. This underscores the tenet that if you look good, you are good. So, if you look professional, you are professional. If you look casual, you are not serious about working.

Take, for example, a young man from California who interviewed for the MSU medical school wearing flip flops . . . in Michigan . . . in January. Even though he had impressive academic credentials and the right letters of recommendation, he blew his chances because his bare feet were a distraction during the interview. The interviewer was focused on the interviewee's lack of attention to wearing the proper attire, in addition to his rather gnarly-looking toenails.

The expression "clothes make the man and the woman" really rings true for job interviews. You can dress the part of a marketing director by buying a new suit, wearing appropriate colors, wearing polished shoes, making sure your hair is in place, getting a manicure, and wearing tasteful jewelry. When you upgrade your appearance, there is a greater likelihood of being hired and an 8 to 20 percent higher projected salary as a result of your upgraded look. Go with recommended dress standards and then personalize your look with a unique pin, brooch, tie, or scarf—nothing outlandish, but something eye-catching that makes you stand out as the unique individual that you are.

Look in the mirror. Are you wearing the appropriate clothing for your scheduled interview? Are you well groomed? Do you have good eye contact and a pleasant smile? Fortunately, you can transform a mediocre appearance into a crazy good one.

The Doctor Is In . . .

"Wear interview attire for a position that's higher than the one you're interviewing for. Wear it a few times before your interview to make sure it's comfortable and doesn't restrict your movements."

Preparation Is Key

Interviewing. Just the thought of it produces nervousness and anxiety. To reduce your pre-interview jitters, devise an interview strategy that will enable you to put your best foot forward. Collectively, your clothing, grooming, body language, and handshake must convey confidence, integrity, and consistency.

Visit your prospective employer's website and learn as much as you can about the company. Do a dry run by driving your car or taking the train or a bus to the job interview site, so you're familiar with the route on the big day, and you know how much travel time is required. Rehearse interview questions with your friends. Practice facial expressions, body language, and try on several interview outfits before you decide on the perfect one.

The Doctor Is In . . .

"Ask a friend to role-play the interview process with you, and videotape it. Watch it to see how you come across, and then make adjustments accordingly."

Your handshake is important, too. Nobody wants to touch a limp, clammy hand. Practice a firm handshake, and hold it for a couple of seconds. If you have a tendency to have sweaty palms, always dry off your hands before your interview. Carry a small hand towel if you have a chronic sweat problem. And, don't frighten off the interviewer with foul breath. Brush your teeth and take a breath mint before you enter the interview arena.

Do not sit down until you are offered a chair. Then, sit tall with squared up shoulders and try to occupy as much space in the chair as possible. Don't be a shrinking violet with a bowed head, no eye contact, and slouching shoulders. By leaving a timid impression, a potential employer will not feel confident about hiring you to tackle assignments that require some chutzpah.

An introduction to someone or your entrance into a meeting or panel interview should convey friendliness. Create a strong likeability factor. Companies hire people they know and like.

Experienced interviewers can smell fear, anxiousness, and, excuse my French, bullshit. The best policy is to just be you, but not "too" you. If you are usually a laid-back person, kick it up a notch, so you do not appear to lack energy or be complacent. If you are normally high strung, try to relax, so you do not resemble a nervous poodle.

The only thing you can do is tell your story easily, effectively, and clearly to influence a positive first impression. Highlight your skills and abilities by saying, "I'm happy to interview for this position, and here are three things I can bring to this job."

When meeting several people at one time, such as during a panel interview, try to involve everyone in the discussion. Direct your comments or questions to all participants, so they can see your sincere interest. Avoid talking about religion, politics, or personal family matters. Only talk about family matters if the interviewer(s) is the first to bring up the subject area, and then you should still exercise caution.

The Doctor Is In . . .

"Don't ramble or try to get chummy. Answer the interviewer's questions succinctly and effectively."

Get Ready to "Act Out"

You probably have heard the term "act out" used to define the release of out-of-control aggressive or sexual impulses to gain relief from tension or anxiety. Young mothers usually say their children are acting out when the little rug rats are having tantrums and are lying on the floor, kicking and screaming.

In this book, the ACT Out strategy is a positive tool for dealing with interview-induced stress. It helps relieve job applicants of the tension and anxiety associated with the dreaded interview process.

It is time to dig in and learn about the ACT Out model to prepare yourself for interviewing successfully, whether it is for admission to a highly competitive school or program, your first job out of college, a career change, or a high-level management position.

The three stages in the ACT Out model are:

1. Assess: Review your strengths and qualifications as they pertain to the position for which you are interviewing.
2. Communicate: Use verbal and non-verbal skills to engage the interviewer.
3. Thank: After the interview, thank the interviewer and stay connected. You should also touch base with your own feelings about the interview and how the job aligns with your career goals.

Chapter 4 will focus on taking inventory of the skills, strengths, and experiences that you bring to the position in question. Specifically, here are some of the key areas that will be addressed:

- What questions should you ask—or not ask—of yourself as well as the interviewer?
- How do you make your top characteristics stand out from other candidates?
- How do you use the rule of three?
- How can you use simple mnemonics to remember what you want to showcase in the interview?
- What is your background and history?
- What is your personal philosophy?
- What makes you unique?

PART I

ACT Out: Assess

4 | Everything from Soup to Nuts

Your Strengths and Limitations

When you were a kid, what did you want to be when you grew up? Did you dream of being a big-time singer, like Frank Sinatra, Elvis, The Beatles, Cindy Lauper, Tina Turner, George Michael, Michael Jackson, Blake Shelton, Carrie Underwood, or Katie Perry? Or were you more idealistic, seeking to serve humanity as a surgeon, teacher, scientist, firefighter, or a police officer? Perhaps you wanted to use your hands, and you envisioned working in construction, carpentry, plumbing, or landscaping. If you liked to tinker, you probably thought about becoming an auto mechanic or an inventor. Or did your daredevil spirit give you aspirations of being a race car driver, an astronaut, or a pilot?

How does what you are doing now differ from what you wanted to do?

No matter what your career dreams were then or now, you need the right tools—talent, education, skills, aptitude, experience, or a combination thereof—to be successful. How do you know you are even cut out for your dream job? In the Assess step of the ACT Out process, you will learn how to identify your strengths and weaknesses; some are easy to determine while others are not.

To put this in the proper context, consider the analogy of being approached by a carnival barker inviting you to Test Your Strength. In this game, participants use a mallet to strike a board with all their might, forcing an object to fly upward and ring a bell. If you ring the bell, you win a prize for yourself or a loved one.

This game is a simple test of physical strength, but how can you assess more difficult areas, such as your personality, skills, competencies, and work background—or teamwork, decision making, and risk taking—and apply them to a vocation? You are not likely to find games that test these particular strengths or limitations at a carnival.

Fortunately, many career-focused self-assessment tools are available on the Internet for free or at a nominal cost. You can search for keywords, like "career-assessment tools" or "personality test," or check out the tests listed below.

You need an accurate assessment of yourself because you will be asked one or more of the following questions at some point in every interview with a potential employer: "Describe yourself in terms of your strengths and weaknesses," "Tell me about yourself and what value you bring to the company," or "How do you think you compare to our other candidates for this position?"

If you can't answer these types of questions at the drop of a hat, your chances for the position sink rapidly.

Assessment Instruments

Self-Assessment Tests

Campbell™ Interest and Skill Survey® (CISS®)

The CISS has been used by career counselors for more than a decade. It was developed by author David Campbell, Ph.D., an expert in career assessment. The test determines your best vocational paths by measuring your interest and confidence within specific skill areas. The test was formerly available to individuals only through licensed counselors, but it is now available online in English and Spanish.

The 320-question survey targets college-bound and college-educated individuals. Your results will be compared to the results of people who are employed in your fields of interest. Your personalized report covers nearly 60 occupations, and helps you interpret the results and plan for your new career.

CareerLeader® www.careerleader.com

CareerLeader is a personalized, online self-assessment that identifies your strengths, weaknesses, skills, passions, and values as they relate to potential career paths within business vocations, including nonprofit management. The tool makes concrete recommendations for your business career path.

Personality and Behavioral Assessment Tools

DISC www.discprofile.com

The Dominant Influential Steady Compliant (DISC) assessment is widely used among companies, human resources professionals, and career counselors. It helps you better understand your behavioral style in the workplace, your ideal work environment, and how others might perceive you.

All people possess characteristics of the following four behavioral types but to varying degrees:

Dominant. Dominant people exhibit control, power, and assertiveness. They can be described as aggressive, determined, and hard-driving, and they actively deal with problems and challenges.

Influential. Influential people are adept in communications and shine in social situations. They are warm, magnetic, convincing, and often base decisions on emotions, rather than data.

Steady. Steady people are patient, persistent, and thoughtful. Their behavior is consistent and predictable. They like security, and they get easily frazzled by change.

Compliant. Compliant people are cautious and follow rules, standards, and guidelines. They like systems and processes, and tend to be neat and exacting.

Myers-Briggs ® Type Indicator (MBTI) www.myersbriggs.org

The MBTI assessment is one of the most well-known personality assessments. The test, which must be given by a qualified test administrator, provides individuals with a personality profile based on 16 common types that result in a combination of four preferences or dichotomies:

1. Extraversion (E) or Introversion (I)
2. Sensing (S) or Intuition (N)
3. Thinking (T) or Feeling (F)
4. Judgment (J) or Perception (P)

Your test result may indicate that you are an extravert-intuition-thinking-judging (ENTJ), an introvert, sensing, feeling, perceiving (ISFP), or one of 14 other combinations. The description can help you identify characteristics of new roles that might suit you.

Skill-Based Assessment

SkillScan™ www.skillscan.com

SkillScan is an interactive tool that will help you identify your natural strengths as they relate to potential careers. Many universities, career counseling practices, and *Fortune* 500 corporations use SkillScan to provide a fast, interactive, and engaging process for identifying transferable skills and applying the results to career planning, career change, professional development, and marketing yourself for your job search.

Ask Your Friends

A relatively easy and simple way to do an assessment of yourself is to ask three to five people who know you well (friends, family members, and co-workers) to provide you with three to five words or phrases that best describe your personality, skills, attributes, and abilities. You can email or text them for their words and phrases.

After receiving their words and phrases, eliminate the negative ones and then look for common clusters of traits. You will probably end up with three to five good descriptions of your strengths. Another benefit of doing this is that you will have a crazy good answer if you are asked "How would your friends describe you?"

Make a List!

If you have been in the workforce for a while, you already have a good idea of what your strengths and weaknesses are. If you are a newcomer to the job market, or you want to switch careers, then you will gain some valuable insights by using a career-assessment tool, like the ones that were just described. It is in your best interests to take stock of your strengths and weaknesses and write them down.

Creating a list of strengths is easy, because everyone likes to be viewed favorably. Here are some common adjectives to describe your strengths as they relate to job performance: assertive, decisive, punctual, honest, precise, methodical, determined, goal-oriented, results-oriented, patient, friendly, collaborative, creative, and the list goes on.

During a job interview, the interviewer will without a doubt ask you to name your top three to five strengths. Pull them from the list you have just created. Always match your strengths with noteworthy and measurable results that you obtained in past positions, and how you can apply those same strengths to your new job situation. Make it easy for the interviewer to picture how you are a good fit for the organization.

Use Mnemonics to Recall Your Strengths

A little forethought and creativity will go far in helping you remember the strengths you want to share in an interview. It helps to write your key words and then look for ways to organize them into a mnemonic. For example, an interviewee can use the classic ABC mnemonic to remember what he/she wants to share with an interviewer, which goes like this:

Use the letter A to stand for something like aptitude, which would stand for a list of skills (e.g., Outlook, Excel, and PowerPoint®) that he/she would be offering the organization. B might be for behaviors, which support the aptitudes (e.g., taking advanced classes in these areas). C could stand for creativity, which would highlight how the candidate used his/her aptitudes in new and novel ways in his/her past work experiences.

A candidate also could use a mnemonic called ACT, standing for (attitude, competencies, and task driven). The interviewee would talk about specific attitudes (typically three) like adaptable, accessible, and action-oriented that he/she would bring to the job. For competencies, the candidate would list at least three areas where he/she has achieved a strong level of achievement (e.g., presentation skills, closing the sale, team player). When talking about being task driven, the candidate would mention how he/she organizes the tasks at hand, plans the steps that need to be taken, and executes these steps.

The three Cs (or most any other letter for that matter) work well, too. Compassionate, concrete, and competitive might be three words that a candidate uses to capture his/her top abilities. Using these three words, the interviewee would give detailed examples of where he/she demonstrated these traits. A crazy good response would then relate these traits to the position: diligent, dedicated, and demanding, or helpful, humble, and handy. You get the idea.

HOMES is used as a mnemonic to remember the Great Lakes (Huron, Ontario, Michigan, Erie, and Superior). A candidate could use it to list adjectives that describe him/herself: honest, open, manageable, eager, studious.

One candidate thought about his three siblings to whom he had attached two characteristics or traits. He then thought of each sibling and talked about the traits associated with that sibling. For example, for his oldest sibling, he recalled leadership and role-modeling characteristics and talked about those traits. For the middle sibling, he talked about negotiation skills and extraversion, and for the youngest sibling, he mentioned traits of exuberance and breaking the rules.

Rate the Behavior

Use the Psychotron to rate the following crazy good and crazy bad responses to the interviewer's question: "How did you use a particular strength to achieve a positive result in your last job?"

Example 1

Crazy good: *"As a regional sales manager, I used my motivational skills to ramp up the sales revenue in my division of 20 sales reps by 60 percent in one year."*

Crazy bad: *"I used my position and scare tactics to drastically increase my sales reps' quotas. Of course, they feared for their jobs and worked their asses off."*

Example 2

Crazy good: *"As a production manager, I used my analytical skills to identify areas where the company could save 40 percent by recycling materials."*

Crazy bad: *"I saved 40 percent by opting for inferior materials in product manufacturing."*

Example 3

Crazy good: *"As a sixth-grade teacher, I used my coaching and training skills to increase my students' scores on a national reading test and move them into the 90th percentile."*

Crazy bad: *"I beat those poor little bastards into submission."*

What's Your Weak Spot?

Admitting your weaknesses can be tricky. All people have them and are reluctant to put themselves in a vulnerable position by confessing their shortcomings. The key is identifying an area that needs improvement and then explaining how you are addressing this area. Ralph Waldo Emerson said it best: "Our strengths grow out of our weaknesses."

What are some of your weaknesses/limitations? Your list might include words like disorganized, perfectionist, lacking in technical expertise, demanding, critical, or whatever your Achilles' heel may be. Interviewers have heard everything under the sun, so your negative quality probably will come as no surprise. All you have to do is spin it in your favor by stating your weakness or limitation, followed by a positive statement.

Rate the Behavior

Using the Psychotron, how would you rate the interview responses below?

Example 1

Crazy good: "I'm not a social media guru, so I enrolled in a workshop to increase my knowledge and understanding of Facebook and LinkedIn."

   Crazy bad: "I don't like using social media at all."

Example 2

Crazy good: "I am trying to improve my public speaking skills, which would be an asset for this position, so I joined Toastmasters."

   Crazy bad: "Give me a few drinks, and I can talk to anyone."

Example 3

Crazy good: "Organizational skills are necessary to be successful in any position. I use a white board and my Outlook planner to keep projects on schedule."

    Crazy bad: "It's a secretary's job to keep my records, correspondence, and schedule up to date." (Note: This response is double crazy bad if the interviewer is a woman, since secretaries traditionally were females.)

A savvy, albeit trickier, approach is to list professional weaknesses that do not even relate to the job you are interviewing for, as shown in these examples:

- "I don't have any artistic ability, but I have always been good with numbers. As your bookkeeper, I am confident that I can keep your spreadsheets balanced to the penny."
- "My sales skills aren't the best, but my top-notch organizational skills are a good match for being your sales team's office support person."

Do not list a weakness or limitation that is not closely related to the position you want, such as the following:

- "Even though I am a poor housekeeper, I am well qualified to be your new bank president." (Not only is this a crazy bad response, it is just plain crazy.)

The Doctor Is In...

"Emphasize your strengths. Minimize your weaknesses. Show how you are working on your limitations."

Human Interaction: Where the Action Is

Human interaction is at the root of every relationship in life, both personal and professional. How well you interact with people is a critical factor in your success and happiness in your job, your love life, and your relationships with family members, neighbors, and even strangers you come into contact with every day.

The word interaction means the combined or reciprocal action of two or more entities or people that have an effect on each other and work together. Like the cyclotron at Michigan State University (MSU), interaction can be weak or strong between elementary particles. The concept of a two-way effect is critical for interaction.

Good human interaction in the workplace promotes a team spirit and keeps employees engaged. Interviewers look for evidence that you can interact well with others and that you will have a positive impact in the workplace. It is not enough to tell the interviewer that you interact well with others. You must provide concrete examples that illustrate your skills and how they produced positive results in your previous positions.

Rate the Behavior

Using the Psychotron, how would you rate the job candidates' behaviors described in the following real-life interviews?

Adults Only

A woman in her mid-30s interviewed for a receptionist position at a mortgage company. She had recently relocated to the area and taken a temporary job as a cashier in an adult bookstore until she could find more appropriate employment. When the interviewer asked about her duties at the store, she responded, "I just moved here and couldn't find anything else. We get our share of weirdoes, but there are some nice, normal customers, too. I don't judge; I just try to help everyone find whatever they're looking for."

Did the applicant exhibit crazy bad behavior for admitting to working in a sleazy adult bookstore, or was it crazy good behavior because, if she could deal with customers buying sex toys and marching in and out of the peepshow rooms, she could provide good customer service to anyone anywhere?

Real-life result: She got the job troubleshooting with bank managers, figuring out their needs, and determining who to direct them to, and she was promoted to a sales representative at the company.

Make the Call

Sometimes an interviewer will ask a job applicant to explain how he or she would handle a hypothetical job situation that involves customer interaction. The response can provide useful information in making a hiring decision, as shown in the following examples:

The director of human resources for a major airline interviewed applicants for a customer relations position. In this real-life situation, she asked four candidates: "How would you handle a difficult caller?"

Candidate 1

"I'd disconnect the call. If anyone asks what happened, I can blame it on system failure."

Candidate 2

"Generally, the airline is right and callers are wrong, so I would argue with the person."

Candidate 3

"I would give the caller some free stuff, such as air miles or a free ticket anywhere in the continental United States."

Candidate 4

"I would listen intently and try to understand the caller's objections, because everyone deserves to be heard. I would try to help the caller based on this input."

Using the Psychotron, which candidate would you hire?

Education: Know Your Own Strengths

Your resume should list your education, including prep schools, private schools, technical schools, junior college, university, post-grad degrees, your class rank, and even the school of hard knocks. If you recently earned your college degree, be prepared to discuss how you selected your major and what you learned in your courses. What skills did you develop in the classroom? Did you work on any special projects that relate to the position? Did you gain any valuable experience?

If your college major differs from the area in which you are now seeking employment, you will need to explain why you are switching career gears and how your major can benefit you in your new field of interest.

You can impress the interviewer by demonstrating ongoing learning through online classes or reading trade publications in your field of interest. An interviewee who has an interest in stock brokerage might tell the interviewer: "I read the *Wall Street Journal* daily to keep a pulse on the financial world."

Jobs that Don't Require College Degrees

Did you know that eight of the 10 fastest growing jobs don't require college degrees, according to the U.S. Bureau of Labor Statistics (BLS)?

Make a list of your job preferences. If any of those jobs do not require a degree, then don't spend money to get a degree just for the sake of earning one.

Do not fret about starting at the bottom, especially if you are new to the job market or you are making a career change. If you do your job well, people will take notice, and you will advance in the organization. In addition, by learning about and working in all phases of a business operation, you set yourself up for business ownership someday. If you start off as a truck driver, you might own the trucking company one day. If you are a hair stylist, you might become a salon owner. If you are hired to clean up construction sites, you could become a foreman or superintendent someday. When you start at a low rung on the ladder, you can work your way to the top in many industries where on-the-job experience supersedes a sheepskin. In fact, two out of every three jobs only require on-the-job training, according to the U.S. Department of Labor.

Check out this list of 19 top careers, with corresponding average annual incomes, that do not require a college degree, according to CNN.

1. Air traffic controller: $102,030
2. Storage and distribution manager: $66,600
3. Transportation manager: $66,600
4. Police and detectives supervisor: $64,430
5. Non-retail sales manager: $59,300
6. Forest fire fighting and prevention supervisor: $58,920
7. Municipal fire fighting and prevention: $58,902
8. Real estate broker: $58,720
9. Elevator installers and repairer: $58,710
10. Sales representative: $58,580
11. Dental hygienist: $58,350
12. Radiation therapist: $57,700
13. Nuclear medicine technologist: $56,450
14. Unemployment insurance fraud investigator: $53,900
15. Criminal investigators and special agent: $53,990
16. Immigration and customs inspector: $53,990
17. Police detective: $53,990
18. Police identification and records officer: $53,990
19. Commercial pilot: $53,870

Skills and Work Experience

On your resume, you should showcase any unusual skills, such fluency in a foreign language, speed reading, sign language, social media expertise, technical aptitude, facilitating webinars, conducting surveys, or public speaking. The interviewer will be keenly interested in a skill that can be applied to the position you are interviewing for, and which can improve efficiency and save time, money, or both, as shown in the following two real-life anecdotes.

Rate the Behavior

Using the Psychotron, how would you rate the job candidate's behavior described in the following real-life interviews?

Upside-Down, Right-Side Up

A man in his 40s applied for a position in flight operations at a major airline. He arrived early for the interview and immediately attracted the attention of the other workers in the office. He was tall, dark, and handsome, and he looked more like a movie star than a prospective airline employee, flashing his gleaming white smile and wearing a well-cut tailored suit.

The human resources director greeted him and ushered him into a small conference room where they took seats across the table from each other. She placed a list of questions in front of her, so the interview could get underway. The applicant glanced over at the page from across the table, read each question aloud, and provided his responses to each one. With his background in military intelligence, he could read the questions upside down faster than the interviewer could read them right-side up.

Did the candidate exhibit crazy bad behavior for taking control of the interview or crazy good behavior because he effectively demonstrated a unique skill that could be an asset to the job he was applying for?

Real-life result: The man was hired, and upper management was pleased with his consistent, stellar performance.

School Daze

A woman in her 30s applied for a position as a receptionist at a real estate company. She had worked in the office at a public high school for many years and simply wanted a change of pace. She had a very pleasant and sweet demeanor, but the interviewer was skeptical about her ability to handle the job. The woman sensed the interviewer's concern and said, "If I can work with unruly high school students who filter in and out of the office all day long and keep them in line, handling the reception desk here will be a piece of cake."

Did the candidate exhibit crazy bad behavior for making an insinuation, or was it crazy good behavior because she tied her job experience to the position she was applying for?

Real-life result: The woman was hired for the position and rose to the rank of office manager.

Accomplishments

If you are new to the workforce or your resume is light on work experience, you can showcase your community involvement, membership in clubs, associations, and charitable organizations, and any special awards or honors you have received that align with your desired career area.

In today's tough economy, interviewers understand that many people experience lapses in employment; however, they will not be sympathetic if you have been doing nothing with your time off. They can only imagine that you have been sitting on your butt and watching TV, playing video games, or sleeping all day long, instead of using your time to be productive, improve your job skills (e.g., social media, computer, or language skills), or dedicate your time to a worthy cause.

Rate the Behavior

Using the Psychotron, how would you rate the following responses to the interviewer's question: "How have you been spending your time since you were laid off work?"

Example 1

Crazy good: "I started a blog about good nutrition for children because my goal is a career as a dietician for a public school district."
    Crazy bad: "I frequent bars in my free time, so I started a blog about the best happy hours in town."

Example 2

Crazy good: "As a Rotary Club member, I helped our chapter raise $10,000 for breast cancer research."
    Crazy bad: "I had breast augmentation since becoming unemployed."

Example 3

Crazy good: "I am taking a class on website development because I want to pursue a career in website design."
    Crazy-bad: "I am following a 12-step program that is confidential in nature."

Areas of Improvement

Even though the goal of the interview is to showcase the positive aspects of your job experience, education, and skills, everyone has one or more weak areas. If you proclaim that you have no areas that need improvement, the interviewer will raise an eyebrow in disbelief or make a mental note of it. It is better to fess up now and look like an honest Abe or Alice.

Could you brush up on your Spanish or French? Hone your organizational skills? Learn how to use your Outlook calendar to schedule appointments? Become savvier about social media? Learn how to create a more dynamic website? Become more proficient in Excel or PowerPoint®?

Rate the Behavior

Using the Psychotron, how would you rate the following responses to the interviewer's question: "In what area(s) do you need improvement?"

Example 1

Crazy good: "I need to brush up on my PowerPoint® skills for my speaking presentations, so I recently signed up for an online class on this topic."

  Crazy bad: "I need to drink more PowerAde after I exercise."

Example 2

Crazy good: "I plan to take a class to improve my business writing skills. I have narrowed my choices to two options."

(continued)

(continued)

Crazy bad: "I plan to focus on Fantasy Football this season to improve my chances of winning."

The Best Policy

If you feel like fudging on your resume to pump up your education or your job experience, my advice to you is simple: Don't. Everything really does come out in the wash. If you have exaggerated your proficiency in a particular skill, people will notice when you appear clueless. If you claimed that you are a computer whiz during the interview, co-workers will wonder why you don't know the most basic functions of Microsoft Office. If you claimed to be fluent in Spanish, why would you refuse to converse over the phone with customers and vendors in Mexico City, Costa Rica, or Spain?

If you are one semester short of earning your bachelor's degree, do not think for one minute that one semester does not matter. If you lie on your resume, chances are good that you will be found out, as the following real-life anecdote illustrates, and the ramifications are not worth the gamble.

Rate the Behavior

Using the Psychotron, how would you rate the job candidate's behavior described in the following real-life anecdote?

Fraud Prevention

A woman in her 30s sailed through the interview process and was hired as a sales manager reporting to the sales director at a luxury hotel. The sales director, who was not part of the interviewing and hiring processes, asked if a background check had been conducted before extending the job offer to her. Upon learning that no one had contacted the woman's references, the sales director took it upon herself to make some calls. She discovered that the woman had misrepresented employment dates on her resume.

Did the candidate exhibit crazy good behavior for fudging on her employment information to get the job, or was it just crazy bad, rotten luck because she was found out?

Results: The human resources director and sales director yanked the woman out of an employee orientation session and fired her on the spot for lying on her application.

The Doctor Is In . . .

"Honesty is the best policy. Always be truthful about your education and employment history . . . or risk public humiliation."

5 | Wild, Wacky, and Wonderful You

What makes you unique?

Will employers remember you as the chatty, multilingual job candidate who worked as a summer camp counselor for physically challenged kids? Are you the upbeat individual who captivated the interviewer with your enthusiasm, proven record of generating sales revenue, and slides of your watercolors? Or are you the quiet brainiac who can solve the Rubik's Cube in seconds and overhauled a company's information technology (IT) network single-handedly?

Your response to this one question is critical during an interview. To tell them who you are, you need to know who you are. In the Assess step of the ACT Out process, you will delve deeply inside yourself to determine the special qualities and talents that make you stand out among other job candidates. If you think there is nothing special about you, think again. You are the only person like you in the whole world, based on a unique combination of three things: biology; your personality, including your enthusiasm, motivation, and interpersonal skills; and your life experiences, including your hobbies and interests, which impact your leadership potential and problem-solving skills.

Biology 101

Don't know much about biology? Then, put your helmet on for a crash course starting with this news flash: Not only are you different from everyone else, you are not even the same person you were six months ago. Nearly every cell of your hair, skin, and bone dies and is continuously replaced by new cells. You make new taste buds every 10 days, new epidermis (outer skin) every two to four weeks, a new stomach lining every five weeks, a new liver every six weeks, and a new skeleton every three months.

You were born with about 100 billion brain cells, the most you'll ever have. But only two areas of the brain regenerate as you age, the areas responsible for smelling and learning. In fact, you may actually lose brain cells as you age, which is the underlying cause of dementia and why head injuries are so devastating.

So, you are probably wondering if there is any part that holds "you" together. Yes, it's your consciousness, where your thoughts and memories are housed.

Let's take a closer look at what makes you different biologically from all other humans on the planet. There are several identifying markers that make every person unique, including DNA, fingerprints, finger length, your voice, and your retina and iris. These markers fall under the field of biometrics.

DNA is the big daddy of identifying markers. You have heard it mentioned on TV dramas, like *Law & Order* and *CSI* when DNA tests are used to solve crimes by positively identifying the perpetrator. DNA testing has gained wide visibility on daytime reality shows, like *Maury* or *Jerry Springer*, to determine paternity, where an unsuspecting and surprised man suddenly learns that he sired a child from a mid-day roll in the hay with his sister-in-law or his best friend's wife. In every episode, you are likely to hear an emotionally charged mother accuse the purported father, "You the baby daddy!" as the audience cheers, "Jer-ry! Jer-ry! Jer-ry!"

Do you know what those three little letters—D–N–A—stand for?

A. Does not apply
B. Do not ask
C. Don't know anything
D. National Dyslexic Association
E. None of the above

The correct answer is: E. None of the above.

In actuality, DNA is deoxyribonucleic acid, a wonderfully complex molecule found in the nucleus of a cell. It contains the genetic code that facilitates the developing and functioning of all living organisms. The genetic code is a proverbial alphabet soup of letters that can be arranged in countless ways. It is so complicated that if the code from all 46 chromosomes were placed end to end, it would be about two meters long. It's confusing to the molecule itself. As one DNA molecule said to another, "I hate being a DNA molecule. I have too much to remember."

Your DNA is different from that of every other person on Earth, unless you have an identical twin. But interestingly, 99.8 percent of your DNA is identical to other humans. That's right, only .02 percent of your DNA accounts for varying human physical characteristics, such as your hair color, eye color, and rate of metabolism. That measly .02 percent of DNA, though, makes you unique from every other person and job applicant in the whole world.

Did you know that your fingers are also highly accurate identifiers of your unique individuality? Shut the front door. Yes, it's true. In fact, Walt Disney World in Orlando, Florida, takes guests' finger measurements to ensure they are using their own ticket each day and not someone else's.

If the subject of genetics floats your boat, you will be interested to know that based on chromosome number, humans are more like potatoes than apes because they both have 46 chromosomes. This is probably how the term couch potato got started. Just ask your bag of chips the next time you're watching TV when you should be fine-tuning your resume or rehearsing your responses to job interview questions.

Personality 101

"You have a great personality."

Unless you are a total schmuck, someone may have told you at one time or another that you have a great personality or at least a good one. People usually associate the word personality with behaviors that make someone socially appealing or unappealing. If you have a great personality, you are viewed as charming, happy, funny, friendly, fun-loving, thoughtful, and people enjoy your company. You are likely to be very popular and have a wide circle of friends. Think cheerleader, homecoming king and queen, the head of the student body, or the life of the party.

On the other hand, if you have a bad personality, you might be described as unfriendly, impatient, sarcastic, rude, boring, or weird, and people will avoid you like the plague. Your social life is zilch, and you will spend your evenings and weekends sitting on the sofa watching TV with your bag of chips. (See reference to couch potato in the Biology 101 section earlier.)

You might be surprised to learn that, from a scientific viewpoint, there is a lot more to personality than outward appearance and actions. It can be defined as a combination of thoughts, emotions, and behaviors that make a person unique. It's a result of genetics and childhood experiences, and it is influenced by gender, birth order, cultural background, family norms, parents' ages, their generational affiliation, socioeconomic background, education, work experience, and many other factors.

The development of the brain also impacts personality development. As the brain develops, you grow connections that impact your decision-making abilities. By the teenage years, your brain has pruned these connections to make it more efficient. Children's decision-making skills are still developing as they move toward their teen years, which, in turn, probably shape other people's impressions of their personality.

Your personality is consistent, and it not only influences how you respond to your environment, it also causes you to act in certain ways. You are likely to behave in the same or similar manner in many different situations. Past behavior is the best predictor of future behavior. Interviewers believe that the ways you handled situations in the past are good indications of how you will handle them in the future.

Carl Jung, whose work is the basis of the Myers-Briggs Type Indicator (MBTI) referenced in Chapter 4, believed that one's personality preferences emerge early in life and are not likely to change. Like left- or right-handedness, individuals are either born with, or develop, certain preferred ways of thinking and functioning.

Introversion versus Extraversion: Are You In or Out?

A major personality indicator is a preference for *extraversion* or *introversion*. (Note: Myers-Briggs prefers the spelling extraversion as opposed to extroversion.) The difference between the two depends on energy creation. Extraverts draw their energy externally through activities, people, and places. They value breadth of experience. They usually have a wide circle of friends and thrive in social situations. They feel drained when they are alone.

Introverts derive their energy from their own thoughts, emotions, and ideas. Introverts are energized by spending time on solitary activities. They are happy when they are reading, creating a work of art, gardening, surfing the Internet, and doing other activities where they can be alone with their thoughts, or in their own heads. They expend energy in social situations, and being around many people for an extended period of time wears them out. They value depth of experience. They need time to be alone and recharge their batteries.

The Doctor Is In . . .

"After a party, extraverts will say they had a great time because they met all 300 people there. Introverts will have a great time, too because they had an in-depth conversation with one person."

The preference for extraversion or introversion is hardwired in the brain. You are born either an extravert or an introvert. To go to the opposite preference requires time, energy, and patience. It is not easy to switch teams. Extraverts and introverts have different brain activity, according to research studies by Debra L. Johnson, of the University of Iowa, and John F. Wiebe, of the University of Texas, which revealed that introverts have more activity (increased blood flow) in the frontal lobes of the brain, the anterior thalamus, and areas of the brain associated with planning and problem solving. Extraverts show more blood flow in the posterior thalamus and areas of the brain associated with the interpretation of sensory data.

Johnson's and Wiebe's research showed that introverts are stimulated internally and the front thalamus helps them to remember, plan, and process their own ideas. Extraverts are stimulated externally and the posterior thalamus attends to their sensory processing (such as listening, watching, or driving) when they are socially active.

Introverts know at any early age they are outnumbered when their teachers tell them that one-third of their grade is based on class participation. They ruminate quietly, "This is unfair." Meanwhile, the extraverts dance with joy and cheer, "How cool is this? If we open our mouths, we can get at least a C!"

The Doctor Is In . . .

"Extraverts comprise 60 to 75 percent of the general population while introverts account for 25 to 40 percent."

Understanding yourself, improving your sensitivity to others, and having an increased understanding of communication styles and preferences are important ingredients for a successful interview. One of the easiest ways to tell introverts apart from extraverts is by their comfort with silence. When you ask a question, extraverts will start speaking before their answer is fully formed, while introverts will wait. Extraverts are very social and will start a conversation with just about anyone. They love to talk. Introverts are more selective and will only talk to people of their own choosing.

Why is this extraversion/introversion preference important? If you are able to determine your interviewer's personality type, you will have an edge in the interview. The following observations can help you to determine the interviewer's preference:

- With an extraverted interviewer, the job candidate should be talkative and animated.
- With an introverted interviewer, the interviewee should reflect on the question in silence, and then respond.
- When two extraverts communicate, they can start a cheerleading squad. But they often end up talking about stuff that has nothing to do with the candidate's qualifications.
- When two introverts communicate, they will be totally in sync but often in silence.
- An introvert and an extravert will get on each other's nerves and will get in each other's way.
- Extraverts speak to find out what is on their minds. This can be troubling to interviewers, especially introverted ones.
- Introverts think in order to speak. The resultant silences where thinking is taking place can be troubling to extraverted interviewers.

The Doctor Is In . . .

"Extraverts tend to answer the interviewer's questions before they are fully asked and often answer the wrong question. Introverts often give short answers and don't feel the need to elaborate. Listen to the entire question, reflect on your answer, and then give a complete response."

Famous Extraverts
Ben Affleck
Sandra Bullock
Johnny Depp
Robert Downey, Jr.
Tom Hanks
Michael Jordan
Martin Luther King, Jr.
Matthew McConaughey
Dr. Phil McGraw
Eddie Murphy

President Barack Obama
Sarah Palin
Anthony Robbins
David Spade
Margaret Thatcher
Donald Trump
Robin Williams
Oprah Winfrey

Although the stereotype of an introvert—shy, reserved, withdrawn, and lacking in social skills—applies to some introverts, many introverts are fun-loving, friendly, likeable, and socially confident. You will be surprised to see many performers among this list:

Famous Introverts
Christina Aguilera
Laura Bush
Johnny Carson
Clint Eastwood
Thomas Edison
Albert Einstein
Eminem
Enya
Harrison Ford
Bill Gates
Mahatma Ghandi
Paris Hilton
Michael Jackson
Billy Joel
John F. Kennedy, Jr.
David Letterman
Abraham Lincoln
George Lucas
Steve Martin
Marilyn Monroe
Sir Isaac Newton
Gwyneth Paltrow

Julia Roberts
Meg Ryan
William Shakespeare
Socrates
Steven Spielberg
Meryl Streep
Mark Twain
Barbara Walters
Tiger Woods

If you have noticed that the list of famous introverts is lengthier than the extraverts' list, there are two logical explanations. First, an overwhelming number of stage performers are introverts. After they are done playing their roles on stage or on TV, they retreat to their dressing rooms to rest and regroup. Second, the Internet is an introvert's best friend. They love to post information which other introverts will find online.

The Doctor Is In...

"What does the extravert want to do after a great party? Find another party or head to a bar. The extravert is charged up and energized. What does the introvert want to do after a great party? Go home, get in bed, pull the covers up, and recharge! Knowing if you have a preference for extraversion or introversion is a crazy good way to get a leg up in the interview."

Interpersonal Skills: Can You Relate?

Now, it's time to get personal, interpersonal, that is. Good interpersonal skills are behavioral skills used to properly interact with others in every area of life, both personal and professional. These skills are often called people skills or soft skills. They are valuable in your relationships with your spouse or partner, siblings, children, friends, neighbors, and in the workplace with supervisors, colleagues, and employees. You need soft skills for daily encounters with people, such as your doctor, dentist, grocery store clerk, auto mechanic, restaurant server, banker, personal trainer, children's teachers, and others.

People with strong interpersonal skills are usually more successful in their professional and personal lives. They are perceived as calm, confident, and charismatic, qualities that are often endearing or appealing to others. In the workplace, positive interpersonal skills increase productivity because conflicts are reduced. People with good interpersonal skills build trust and confidence, and they can work effectively on teams or in leadership roles. They respond appropriately in difficult situations and can perform under pressure in a fast-paced environment without crumbling or going psycho.

Your interactions with co-workers can have a dramatic impact on your career, as well as on your day-to-day life. You may be brilliant at your job, but if you can't get along with your colleagues, you won't climb the corporate ladder. If your interpersonal skills are marginal, it might be time to brush up on them. Typically, interpersonal skills fall into the following categories:

Listening skills. The ability to listen actively, which can improve personal relationships by reducing conflicts, strengthening cooperation, and fostering understanding.

Communication skills. The ability to effectively deliver a clear message in a respectful way that has been received and properly understood.

Assertiveness. The ability to directly express your ideas and opinions while considering the needs of others.

Decision making. The ability to determine the proper course of action after evaluating the risks.

Stress management. The ability to manage and respond to stress to prevent or minimize negative physical, mental, and emotional symptoms.

Verbal communication. The ability to use words, either spoken or written, to convey a message.

Non-verbal communication. The ability to send and receive wordless messages via body language, posture, facial expressions, eye contact, and gestures.

The Doctor Is In . . .

"The candidates who demonstrate the strongest interpersonal skills will often receive a job offer even if they don't have the best job experience because they make a great first impression."

Your Assignment

Take out a sheet of paper and divide it into six categories: communications skills, assertiveness, decision making, stress management, verbal communication, and nonverbal communication. For each category, write down the words, adjectives, and phrases that you would use to describe yourself. Next, jot down the words, adjectives, and phrases that others would use to describe you in each category. Think hard about what people have said about you or what has been written about you in past performance appraisals. After you compile your two lists for each category, look for words, phrases, and adjectives that are common to both. This is useful information for assessing your overall interpersonal skills and identifying areas for improvement. Don't just think about the words and phrases that describe you. Commit the words to paper. In this way, they will sink in.

Do not despair if you think you cannot win any popularity contests. There are ways you can improve how others perceive you, such as acting friendly, keeping a positive attitude, being a good listener, showing genuine interest in others, and lavishing praise on co-workers and colleagues for their performance, when warranted.

Enthusiasm and Motivation: Rah-Rah, Sis-Boom-Bah!

If you were an employer, would you rather hire a lackluster candidate or someone who oozes enthusiasm? It's a no-brainer that companies are drawn to energetic and motivated applicants because enthusiasm is contagious. These individuals are more likely to take initiative, explore challenges, and motivate other employees with their positive attitudes.

Employers look for people who convey a sense of excitement and a willingness to go beyond for the company, and possess tenacity to reach goals, complete tasks and objectives, and forge ahead even when the going gets tough. When people are excited about their jobs and believe their function is critical to the organization, they will have enthusiasm for its products and services.

The Doctor Is In . . .

"Psychometrics is the term for standardized psychological tests that are proven and valid measures of personality, ability, aptitude, and interest."

Numerous personality tests—called psychometric tests—are available online and can assess your motivation, attitude, and preferred way of doing things. Test results help employers match candidates to jobs. These types of tests usually are not timed, and there are no right or wrong answers, so don't guess which answers the employer wants. Answer truthfully, but don't over-think your answers, as your initial response will be the most accurate representation of yourself.

Interview Question

Why do you feel you can be successful in this position?
Crazy good: I have the skills necessary to succeed in this position.
(Then tell a brief story to prove it.) I am energetic and willing to learn.
Previous employers will attest to the fact that I am a very hard worker.

What words, adjectives, and phrases would you use to describe your enthusiasm and motivation? What words, adjectives, and phrases would *others* use to describe your enthusiasm? Think about what people have said about you, or what has been written about you in past performance appraisals. After you compile your two lists, look for words, phrases, and adjectives that are common to both. This is useful information for assessing your overall enthusiasm and motivation and identifying areas for improvement. Just as in the section on Interpersonal Skills, it is important that you commit this information to paper.

Think of instances in which you had to effuse enthusiasm, or your motivation inspired others on your team. It will be handy for you to have an anecdote or two in your hip pocket, just in case the interviewer raises the question.

Problem Solving: What's Your Problem?

Every day people are faced with problems with employees or co-workers in the workplace, or with spouses, children, siblings, and parents at home. You might as well face it: Problems are part of life, but the sailing will be a lot smoother if you know how to handle them when they arise. Good problem-solving skills will help you get ahead on the job and on the home front. Your ability to analyze and synthesize information in order to reach a rational and logical solution is an asset when stating your value-add to prospective employers.

How are your problem-solving skills? Think of instances when you were faced with personal or corporate challenges. How did you overcome these situations? What specific personality traits have helped you tackle problematic situations successfully?

When a problem rears its ugly head, do you face it head on, or do you head for the nearest escape hatch and bury your head in the sand, like Daniel, actor Robin Williams' character in the movie *Mrs. Doubtfire*?

Daniel: *How about we take a vacation, take the kids, get you away from work? You'll see that you're a different person. You are. You're great.*

Miranda: *But our problems would be waiting for us when we got back.*

Daniel: *Well, we'll move, and, hopefully, our problems won't follow us.*

Organizations want to hire employees who have good problem-solving skills, such as the ability to prioritize tasks, research and analyze problems, apply troubleshooting techniques, and resolve routine work problems, such as customer complaints. When asked how you solve problems in the workplace, pull this rabbit out of your hat. It's always good to have some pat responses up your sleeve.

Crazy good: My problem-solving process consists of collecting relevant data, identifying the problem, determining the cause, evaluating potential solutions, selling the solution to stakeholders and, finally, implementing it.

If you are a newbie to the job market, you can assess your problem-solving skills by taking any of the self-tests available on the Internet. You can bet your boots that a prospective employer will ask how you solved a problem in the workplace. Prepare to have some anecdotes in your back pocket.

What words, adjectives, and phrases would you use to describe your problem-solving skills? What words, adjectives, and phrases would *others* use to describe your problem-solving skills? Think about what people have said about you, or what has been written about you in past performance appraisals. After you compile your two lists, look for words, phrases, and adjectives common to both. This is useful information for assessing your overall problem-solving skills and identifying areas for improvement.

Think of instances in which your problem-solving skills produced a positive result. It will be handy for you to have an anecdote at the ready, just in case the interviewer raises the question.

Creativity: Thinking Outside the Box

Creativity extends beyond artistic endeavors, such as drawing, painting, and sculpting; musical talents, such as playing the piano, guitar, or other instruments; composing scores; writing lyrics; or penning novels or children's books. Creativity is the ability to generate novel and useful ideas and apply them to everyday problems and challenges.

As competition gets stronger, organizations realize that it's increasingly necessary to find innovative approaches to business problems. They may look for this creativity in their staff, or they may even recruit more creative employees who can bring fresh perspectives and solutions to problems, and identify ways to improve processes. This approach helps market the organization, so it can be viewed as cutting edge and be known for its edgy innovative staff. It can increase productivity and efficiency by solving current problems and eliminating business obstacles. In business, creativity can launch major projects or handle minor snafus. Your creativity can fuel fresh insights and new perspectives on routine tasks. Learning to use your creativity will rekindle your spark in your work, increase your confidence in facing problems head on, and take advantage of the creative input of others.

What's the QT on Your CQ?

For each statement about your Creativity Quotient (CQ), answer with the following: always, sometimes, or never.

1. I do not like to stick to old methods and ideas.
2. I am always looking for ways to apply my creativity.
3. I believe in pushing the envelope and daring to be different.
4. My mind is always whirling with ideas and solutions.
5. I find work boring unless I can use my creativity.
6. I prefer working with creative types, rather than people who follow rules to the letter.
7. I must be challenged to use my imagination regularly.
8. I tend to avoid instructions and directions that are too inflexible.
9. I must be given opportunities to apply my creativity.
10. I cannot work in a rigid and restrictive environment.
11. I can think on my feet and find creative solutions quickly.
12. Most people describe me as creative.
13. People seek me out for my creative solutions.
14. People think my ideas are over the top.
15. People resist my ideas at first, but eventually see the methods to my madness.

Tally your score. If you have an abundance of "always," then you are oozing in creativity. If your answers are predominantly "sometimes," then your creativity falls into the middle range, and there are some areas where you can improve. If your responses are mostly "never," then you probably aren't that creative, but it's never too late to start thinking outside the box.

What words, adjectives, and phrases would you use to describe your creativity? What words, adjectives, and phrases would *others* use to describe your creativity? Think about what people have said about you, or what has been written about you in past performance appraisals. After you compile your two lists, look for words, phrases, and adjectives that are common to both. This is useful information for assessing your overall creativity and identifying areas that could use some improvement.

Think of some instances in which you used your creativity to solve a problem, took an unusual approach to projects, or looked through a different lens. It will be handy for you to have an anecdote or two stashed at the ready, just in case the interviewer raises the question.

Life Experiences 101

Leadership: Follow the Leader. . . or Be One

Organizations seek leaders or employees who have leadership potential. Leadership and management skills are indications of your potential to rise in the company. Leaders encourage their co-workers and teammates to succeed. They take charge and guide discussions. Psychologists debate whether these skills are natural inclinations or learned qualities because not everyone is cut out to be a leader and academic success does not ensure leadership success.

What are the qualities of a good leader?

Lead by example. Good leaders show co-workers or team members that they are willing to roll up their sleeves and pitch in to help finish the job or project.

Passion. A leader without passion is a taskmaster. When leaders are passionate in what the organization is trying to accomplish, their passion is contagious.

Well-organized. Being well-organized breeds productivity and serves as an example to others.

Delegate. A good leader delegates responsibility, tells employees what is expected, and then leaves it up to them to produce results. This instills a feeling of ownership in employees.

Take ownership and responsibility. After delegating to employees, a good leader takes ownership and responsibility for the big picture at all times.

Communicate effectively. Good leaders talk and listen. Keeping people motivated means listening, asking questions, and understanding their issues. They also communicate to employees how their work matters in the bigger picture.

Tell it like it is. Good leaders present things to the team in an honest and direct manner.

People connectors. Good leaders take a personal interest in people and know what makes them tick.

Leaders also follow. Great leaders are great followers, too. They are inspired by their team.

Take note that not all leaders are extraverts; many of the best leaders are introverts.

Lead, Follow, or Get Out of the Way Quiz

Read each statement and answer always, sometimes, or never as it applies to you.

1. I am usually in charge of group assignments in the workplace.
2. People often look up to me and my values.
3. When I fail, it makes me want to try even harder.
4. I challenge myself to exceed personal goals.
5. I have friendly, but professional, relationships with superiors, co-workers, and subordinates.
6. I take the initiative in a group setting.
7. I am comfortable speaking in front of a group of people.
8. I always finish what I start.
9. People describe me as a goal-oriented person.
10. I like to make all of the decisions in my personal and professional lives.
11. People describe me as a people person.
12. I am usually designated as the team leader in the workplace.
13. I am good at handling pressure and stress.
14. I adapt easily to change, new people, and new ideas.
15. I am diplomatic when presenting my views.
16. I am knowledgeable in my field of work.

Tally your score. If you have an abundance of always, then your leadership ability is on par with General Patton. If your answers are predominantly sometimes, then your leadership skills fall into the middle range, and there are some areas where you can improve. If your responses are mostly never, then you probably aren't a born leader, but hey, there's nothing wrong with being a good follower.

What words, adjectives, and phrases would you use to describe your leadership skills? What words, adjectives, and phrases would *others* use to describe your leadership skills? Think about what people have said about you, or what has been written about you in past performance appraisals. After you compile your two lists, look for words, phrases, and adjectives that are common to both. This is useful information for assessing your overall leadership skills and identifying areas for improvement.

Think of some instances in which you had to use your leadership skills. Prepare an anecdote or two that illustrate your leadership, just in case the interviewer expresses interest. Your interviewers will salute you.

Hobbies and Interests: What Do You Do in Your Spare Time?

Interviewers may ask, "Do you have any hobbies or special interests?" Although this question may seem odd during an interview, employers have a good reason for inquiring. By definition, a hobby is a pursuit outside your regular occupation. It gives the employer a broader perspective of you and sheds light on your personal life. This is an area where you can shine, particularly if you have a unique interest. How you spend your leisure time reflects your passions in life. In today's job market, interject your personality into the interview, so you can stand apart.

You also may have some transferable skills—skills acquired through your hobbies or volunteer work—that can be applied to your next job or a new career. For example, if you played team sports, such as softball, volleyball, basketball or football in high school or college, you learned to look out for your teammates. In the workplace, this experience would translate to covering for co-workers in the office or on the trading floor.

> *Crazy good: As the quarterback on my college football team, I learned to watch out for the other guy.*
>
> *Crazy bad: My hobbies? Recreational drugs and finding new bars to frequent.*

In addition to being useful to career changers, transferable skills are important to those who are facing a layoff, new graduates who are looking for their first jobs, and to those re-entering the workforce after an extended absence.

If you have a keen interest in your hobby, consider the possibility of turning it into a career. Do you love gardening, taking care of animals, dancing, or hiking? Have you ever wondered what it would be like if you could spend more time on your hobby and less time at work? Maybe it's not an either/or situation. Perhaps you can do both at the same time.

This is a partial list of popular hobbies and interests and how you can apply them to talents and skills required in the workplace. For example, if you are a marathon runner, your personality trait is to complete projects regardless of obstacles. Here are more examples:

- If you like to cook, you have a creative side and can improvise when not all ingredients are at hand.
- If you like to fish, you are a very patient and focused. You could be good with children or working with elderly people.
- If you are a chess player, then you might be savvy at developing business strategies.
- If you are an athlete, you may be aggressive in achieving sales goals or annual sales targets.
- If you are actively involved in community groups, you may have some managerial potential.
- If you like playing Scrabble or doing crossword puzzles, you probably have a broad vocabulary and perhaps some untapped writing skills.
- If you're an avid reader, you have a thirst for knowledge and might be a good researcher.
- If you sell your handmade crafts, you may have a business head for selling other products.

- If you have several pets, you can apply your love of animals in a job as a veterinary assistant or become a veterinarian.
- If you were a summer camp counselor, then you may have good leadership skills.
- If you like to build computers, you have the aptitude to be an IT tech.
- If you like to shoot skeet or hunt, you may be qualified to enter the police academy.
- If you know karate or judo or belong to a fight club, you may qualify as a bodyguard or a prison guard.

Rate the Behavior

A candidate applied her experience as a volleyball player to the skills needed for a medical residency. Using the Psychotron, how would you rate her behavior in the following real-life interview?

Netting a Job Offer

She was an avid volleyball player, loved the sport, and played whenever she could.

When it came time for her interview, for a very competitive medical residency position, she thought she might be able to use her knowledge and experience in volleyball.

She told the interviewer, "I have had many experiences that capture who I am and what I would bring to your program, but volleyball captures me best. I thrive as a setter, hitter, blocker, libero, and teammate."

Then, she used each of these terms and roles as a metaphor for what she would bring to this position. As a setter in volleyball, she was comfortable as a leader and listener. As a hitter, she was assertive and decisive. As a blocker, she knew how to build trust and communication. As a libero, she could demonstrate flexibility and anticipation. Finally, as a teammate, she would show her dedication and hard work. She then elaborated on each role and provided examples of where these accompanying traits had served her well.

Coincidentally, one of her interviewers had a daughter who played volleyball, knew what a libero was, and was interested in her qualifications.

Was her behavior crazy good for taking a chance on relating her abilities to volleyball, or was it crazy bad for using a sports metaphor that might turn off her interviewers, especially those who are not interested in sports?

Real-life result: She aced her interviews and got the position.

By letting the interviewer know you give back to the community, it sends the message that you are an unselfish team player and would be a good corporate citizen. You give your time and expertise without expecting a paycheck or a pat on the back. HR managers keep their eyes and ears open when job candidates mention special skills that can be applied to the organization's charitable efforts. For example, if you have carpentry skills, the hiring manager may take note that you may be a good addition to the organization's Habitat for Humanity volunteer initiative.

> **Crazy good:** *I donate my time and expertise in drawing blood at the local blood bank.*
>
> **Crazy bad:** *I donate blood. Fifteen gallons, so far.*

Focus your answer on productive applications of your work-related skills. Don't get sidetracked describing a cause that does not demonstrate job-related skills. Avoid discussing any charity or organization that may be considered controversial.

Make a list of all of your hobbies and interests. Before each interview, review your list to see if any of them apply to the job. Always connect your hobby or interest to the job you want to land.

> *Crazy good: My experience as a youth leader at the local YMCA has taught me leadership and teamwork that can be utilized in the role as sales manager.*
>
> *Crazy bad: "I play a lot of trivia games. I am an overflowing fountain of worthless knowledge, which would make me perfect as a research assistant."*

Chapter 5 has shown you how to identify all of the components of your biology, your personality, and your life experiences that fit together magically to form a one-of-a-kind masterpiece titled "Wild, Wacky and Wonderful You."

You are armed with great information, some that you probably weren't even aware of when you started reading this chapter. Truly, you are like a Haley's comet, a unique constellation of attributes. (Don't credit me with this clever turn of phrase; I borrowed it from the movie, *Must Love Dogs*.) Now, you can matriculate to Chapter 6 and learn how to use this knowledge to create your Unique Value Proposition (UVP), the most powerful tool in your arsenal, and the secret to successfully selling yourself in an interview.

6 | Selling "Crazy": Your Unique Value Proposition

If you've made it to the interview stage, do not fool yourself into thinking that you are the only job candidate. At least a half dozen other qualified people are going to be interviewed for the same position. How can you stand out? What is so irresistibly and unequivocally unique about you that you will blow an interviewer's hair back in today's job market?

In Chapter 5, you learned how to assess all of the components that make you one-of-a-kind, including your biological make up, your personality, enthusiasm and motivation, interpersonal skills, problem-solving skills, creativity, and the transferable skills from your hobbies and special interests. How do you slice and dice this information and wrap it into a nice, neat package that's a compelling statement about you and the value you offer? How can you attract the interest of employers who are sifting through stacks of job applications or countless emails with resume attachments? How can you convince the hiring manager that you are a perfect fit for the position? How can you solve the department's, company's, or business's problem?

The answer is to develop your unique value proposition (UVP), also called a personal branding statement. In this book, we will use UVP. It should be one sentence that describes you with razor-sharp clarity. It sets the stage for further discussion of your skills, your strengths, and the extra value you can bring to the company.

Think "Log Line"

In Hollywood, screenwriters craft a log line, one powerful sentence about their screenplays that captures a studio's or director's attention amid a slush pile of unsolicited scripts. It states the main concept or plot of the story and provides an emotional hook in one or two concise sentences. A log line is not a tagline like one that goes on a movie poster. For example, the poster tagline "Don't go in the water" says nothing about the story plot for the movie, *Jaws*.

A clear log line gets Hollywood agents or producers excited about reading the script, just as your UVP will get interviewers or hiring managers sitting on the edge of their seats to learn more about you. Crafting a log line is a screenwriter's first step in planning a screenplay, and writing a UVP should be the first step in a job hunter's interview strategy. You must be prepared with this statement before you even walk into the interview. When the interviewer shakes your hand, offers you a seat, and then says, "Tell me about yourself," you can immediately pull this line out of your arsenal. Instantly, you will impress the interviewer with your preparedness and clarity, compared with other candidates who ramble with no direction.

Writing a log line for a movie script is not as easy as it would seem. It can be very difficult for a writer to extract the essence of the story in one or two sentences. The following log lines describe, in a nutshell, the central focus of these box-office hits:

- Not even a Great War can stand between a boy and his beloved horse. (*War Horse*)
- A family, including a young couple, travels to Paris, France, for business and have their lives transformed. (*Midnight in Paris*)
- New York cop John McClane gives terrorists a dose of their own medicine as they hold hostages in an L.A. office building. (*Die Hard*)

- A seventeenth century tale of adventure on the Caribbean Sea where the roguish yet charming Captain Jack Sparrow joins forces with a young blacksmith in a gallant attempt to rescue the Governor of England's daughter and reclaim his ship. (*Pirates of the Caribbean*)
- Toula's family has exactly three traditional values: "Marry a Greek boy, have Greek babies, and feed everyone." When she falls in love with a sweet, but WASPy guy, Toula struggles to get her family to accept her fiancée while she comes to terms with her own heritage. (*My Big, Fat, Greek Wedding*)
- A young man and woman from different social classes fall in love aboard an ill-fated voyage at sea. (*Titanic*)
- After a series of grisly shark attacks, a sheriff struggles to protect his beach community against the blood-thirsty monster, in spite of the greedy chamber of commerce. (*Jaws*)
- Aliens try to invade earth on Independence Day. (*Independence Day*)
- An attorney, because of his son's birthday wish, can't tell any lies for 24 hours. (*Liar, Liar*)
- An archeologist is hired by the U.S. government to find the Ark of the Covenant before the Nazis. (*Raiders of the Lost Ark*)
- When a Roman general is betrayed, and his family is murdered by an insane and corrupt prince, he comes to Rome as a gladiator to seek revenge. (*Gladiator*)
- In a future where criminals are arrested before the crime occurs, a cop struggles on the lam to prove his innocence for a murder he has not yet committed. (*Minority Report*)

Successful companies around the world have developed their own log lines, which are UVPs for their products and services. In business, a UVP is synonymous with a unique sales proposition (USP). You will hear these terms used interchangeably. UVPs describe—in a succinct manner—why customers should buy from these companies. Every organization needs one to articulate its value in the marketplace. The following are some very famous UVPs:

Amazon: Low price, wide selection with added convenience anytime, anywhere.
Avis: We're number two. We try harder.
BMW: The ultimate driving machine.

Domino's Pizza: You get fresh, hot pizza delivered to your door in 30 minutes or less or it's free. (This is an excellent UVP because it states specific benefits *and* the guarantee.)

Fed Ex: When your package absolutely, positively has to get there overnight.

Michael Jackson: The King of Pop.

M&Ms: The milk chocolate melts in your mouth, not in your hand.

Create Your Unique Value Proposition

If log lines work in Hollywood, and UVPs work in the business world, you certainly can apply this same strategy to prepare for job interviews. Your UVP tells potential employers why they should hire you when everyone else is jumping up and down, waving their arms, and yelling, "Pick me! Pick me!" Your UVP's underlying message is that the employer will receive more value for the money if they hire you and not the other job candidates.

Before you put pen to paper, or fingertips to keyboard, consider your strengths and how they can help the employer produce greater quality, improve efficiency, enhance customer service, or promote product/service leadership and innovation. Connect your abilities and experience with the organization's needs and objectives. Focus on the benefits you can produce and provide examples how you have done so in the past to enhance credibility. Think from the employer's perspective and continually keep it in mind.

A killer UVP prompts interviewers to ask more questions. Instead of saying, "I'm a marketing consultant" or "marketing expert," you must tell what you can do that begs the question from the interviewer, "Can you do that for this organization, too?"

A powerful UVP inspires, engages, and consists of three parts:

1. **Unique:** Who are you? What is unique about you, your values, your approach, and your methods? Do you have a niche that appeals to some employers and not others? If so, this is a crazy good thing.
2. **Value:** What is your biggest strength, the meaningful worth of what you offer to your intended audience? What is your intrinsic worth? By being clear about your value, you can connect with companies

that share those values. Can they benefit from your skills, talents, experience, and competencies?

3. **Proposition:** What can you deliver consistently? Your proposition is a promise that you can consistently deliver on your value. Use supporting evidence, including anecdotes of your achievements and success stories, reports, portfolios, and measurable results. If you can't keep your promise, change it.

This crazy good UVP incorporates all three elements:

"I'm a seasoned IT manager with extensive systems experience that has resulted in upgrading and streamlining networks and saving over $1.3 million for LMN Company in the past five years."

Congratulations. The job candidate just succeeded in piquing the interviewer's attention. Her ears have perked up and she is leaning forward to hear more. Now, the candidate can proceed in explaining how he or she can achieve similar results for the interviewer's company.

Here are two more crazy good UVPs:

"As a third-grade teacher specializing in reading, I was able to increase my students' national test scores by more than 20 percent in the second semester alone."

"I'm a seasoned magazine managing editor with experience in requests for proposals (RFPs), which resulted in saving the publisher 33 percent in printing and mailing costs last year."

The Doctor Is In . . .

"Your UVP articulates your value to an organization and to yourself."

It's your turn to write your own UVP. If you can't articulate your value and write it down on paper, then potential employers will have trouble understanding what makes you unique and will be unable to connect your value to the organization. Your value is the intrinsic worth of everything you offer to employers; it defines what they get for their money.

You already know how you are different from others, based on the personal information you gleaned in Chapter 5. Refer to your existing list or make a new list of all of the things that clearly distinguish you from other job contenders. If you have insider knowledge about the organization, try to familiarize yourself with some jargon that floats their boat, like "profitability" or "quality customer care" or "return on investment" and incorporate it into your UVP. If possible, quantify your UVP with time or financial stats, as shown in the IT manager's UVP two paragraphs ago.

Your UVP is what you bring to the table professionally or personally, whether it's a history of exceeding sales goals or convincing your sweetheart to build a future with you. A clear vision will steer your path in life. It will change continually and should be modified as you acquire more skills, work experience and achievements, or decide to take a new direction. Everyone has heard stories about people who achieve corner-office status, and then suddenly realize it's not what they want in life and does not make them feel fulfilled.

Your Five-Sentence Personal History

You can support your UVP with a five-sentence personal history, which identifies your top three to five strengths in areas like technical skills, transferable skills, and your personal positive traits, such as your ability to meet deadlines or always having a positive attitude. Before each interview, review the requirements listed in the job posting and adapt your strengths to demonstrate that you are a good match. If the ad specifies "a team player with good communication and organizational skills," work that phrase into your personal history. Other popular phrases among employers in today's economy are: people skills, time management, project management, branding, and cost reduction. Two big buzz phrases are social media and social networking. Be sure to use these terms, if applicable and whenever possible.

This five-sentence infomercial is your personal brand. If it helps, write out specific examples of your skills and accomplishments as they relate to your strengths. Include the keywords in the job posting or the organization's preferred jargon if you know it (e.g., profitability, quality customer care, and return on investment). This exercise prepares you to show the interviewer that you have experience in these areas, and you are head and shoulders above your competition in the job market.

Your infomercial could include the following elements, some of which you unearthed during your self-discovery in Chapter 5:

- Your area(s) of expertise
- Your strengths
- Your work ethic
- Your education, training, certifications
- Past performance appraisals
- Personal traits

Following are two crazy good examples of five-sentence personal histories that will make dynamite impressions on the interviewers.

Example 1

"I grew up in the Midwest in a family with two siblings (one older brother and one younger sister). My parents both worked and taught us the values of hard work, discipline, and communicating openly with one another. I attended ABC College, where I majored in business and worked part-time at the DEF Ad Agency during my undergraduate years to pay my tuition. After graduating with honors, my first job was in the loan department at GHI National Bank where I learned the basics of mortgage lending, and I ranked in the top ten percent of the department over the next three years. I am interested in this position because I know I can utilize my sales, marketing, and people skills to take the next step in my career and to advance the goals of this organization."

Example 2

"If I could choose three words that capture what I can bring to this job, they would be engineer, athlete, and fund-raiser. I have always been interested in how things works, which led to a degree in mechanical engineering at JKL University. I have always been active because growing up in Texas taught me the value of being healthy. I believe in giving back to my current community, and I am involved in fund raising for worthy causes. From these three areas, I have developed a set of skills that include creative thinking, enthusiasm, and teamwork."

Why Anecdotes Work

Your career success stories can bridge the gap between your unique abilities and related situations in a new job. Although it may be a new industry or job you are pursuing, there are many similarities in the day-to-day challenges and opportunities. You can stand out from the competition by telling stories or anecdotes that illustrate your previous professional or life experiences. Anecdotes clothe the bare bones of your resume or job application.

Everyone has a story to tell and, believe me, anecdotes can be even more effective than statistics in a job interview. People remember stories; they forget numbers. People connect emotionally with anecdotes; they gloss over statistics. Faced with a story, people take action; faced with data, people nod off or let the information go in one ear and out the other. A good story can liven up an interview and reveal your personality. It's important to convey your personality during an interview, rather than come across as just another cookie-cutter candidate.

Even the President of the United States uses anecdotes to create an emotional connection with his audience and make a point. In his State of the Union address on January 25, 2011, President Barack Obama shared an anecdote about Kathy Proctor, a hard-working American student at Forsyth Tech in North Carolina, who embodies the spirit of a major issue in today's economy:

"One mother of two, a woman named Kathy Proctor, had worked in the furniture industry since she was 18 years old," President Obama said. *"And she told me she's earning her degree in biotechnology now, at 55 years old, not just because the furniture jobs are gone, but because she wants to inspire her children to pursue their dreams, too. As Kathy said, 'I hope it tells them to never give up.'"*

By telling this story, President Obama put a human face on an important issue that has affected the whole nation. Job candidates can use this same strategy by peppering the interview with anecdotes to highlight their personality, form an emotional connection with hiring managers, and stand out from other candidates. Every story you tell gives people an insight into who you are: resilient, methodical, patient, and creative. When job seekers use stories effectively, they also demonstrate their communication skills to employers.

Three Ways to Punch Up Anecdotes

1. Be specific. Instead of saying, "I worked at a company that sold computer software," say "When I was a manager at Microsoft...."
2. Tell about a specific individual who achieved something after overcoming an obstacle. (Of course, you were instrumental in the victory.) Instead of saying, "In 2011, the accounting team was facing a problem," say "In 2011, I helped Joe Smith in accounting overcome a problem with...."
3. Paint a picture. Engage the interviewer by using vivid details. Instead of saying, "We restructured the graphic arts department to better meet client deadlines...," say "Our graphics team had trouble meeting deadlines for our client in Japan, so I reconfigured schedules to prevent tense, high-pressure situations, submit projects in a timely manner, and keep the client happy."

Anecdotes liven up interviews and make you human to the interviewer. Prepare a few anecdotes in advance that highlight certain skills, talents, and qualities, rather than hoping one will pop into your brain on the big day. At a minimum, you should have an anecdote for each of the following topics:

- Dealing with challenging co-workers.
- Handling difficult customers/clients to resolve an issue.
- Averting a disaster in the workplace.
- Dealing with a high-pressure situation.

When the interviewer asks you a question, use an anecdote to support and illustrate the supporting evidence behind your response. Your anecdote should follow the "situation–action–result" model, as shown in the following example:

An interviewer asked three job candidates: "Did you ever comfort an employee who felt unjustly treated by a co-worker?"

Candidate 1

"I got sucked into my co-worker's ongoing drama and it was an utter nightmare. Never again."

Candidate 2

"Yes, I listened patiently while he vented his frustration."

Candidate 3

"Yes, my co-worker was upset because her supervisor asked her to stay late every day until her work was done. I offered to help her with the workload, and now we both leave on time."

Which candidate left the most lasting and favorable impression? Hint: The third response told a story that has value and makes a statement about the job candidate.

For each appropriate interview question, relate it to a similar situation earlier in your career, talk briefly about how you handled it, and highlight the results. These stories demonstrate to the interviewer that you have specific experience dealing with similar situations.

For example, the interviewer might ask you, "How do you deal with high-pressure situations?" You could simply answer: "I'm very good when faced with high-pressure situations. I had to deal with them daily at my last job." This response, however, is very general and does not convince the interviewer of your abilities. Instead, use a career success story:

"When I led my team of sales reps to become the top sales team in the country for our organization last year, we did not make the top 10 in the third quarter. So, I organized a sales retreat to motivate the team, identify our prospects, determine goals for each individual rep, and figure out how we—as a team—were going to snag the coveted number one spot. The result: My sales team exceeded sales goals by 75 percent. We were recognized as the top sales team in the country, and received sizeable bonuses for our efforts."

The Power of Three

In a job interview, you have a secret weapon called the "power of three." The concept of "three" might even have mystical powers (think Holy

Trinity). It is at the cornerstone of the arts and used widely in literature, film, and music, as shown in the following examples:

Children's stories: *The Three Musketeers, Goldilocks and the Three Bears, The Three Little Pigs*
TV shows: *Three's Company, The Three Stooges, My Three Sons*
Movies: *The Three Amigos, Three Men and a Baby, Three Days of the Condor*
Songs: *Three Times a Lady* (The Commodores), *Two Out of Three Ain't Bad* (Meat Loaf), *Three Little Birds* (Bob Marley)
Famous threesomes: Moe, Larry, and Curly; Tom, Dick, and Harry; Winkin', Blinkin', and Nod

What is the power of three? People tend to remember things in threes, perhaps because we have three brains (e.g., reptilian, limbic, and neo-cortex). We like two things, elements, or entities to be connected by a third. We tend to divide things into three categories, including the following:

- Time: past, present, and future
- Direction: left, right, straight ahead
- Size: small, medium, large
- Temperature: low, medium, high

The power of three can be applied to job interviews. It is a highly effective technique for answering an interviewer's open-ended questions like these:

- What skills do you bring to this position?
- What are your top strengths?
- What relevant experiences have prepared you for this job?
- Where do you see yourself in 10 years?
- Tell me about yourself.

The power of three demonstrates that the candidate has the ability to select, condense, and convey what he/she wishes to share with an interviewer. For example, when the interviewer says, "Tell me about yourself," you can describe yourself personally, academically, and professionally. Within each of these categories, you can list three traits. (Remember to use acronyms as simple mnemonic devices as explained in Chapter 4.)

To really stand out among other candidates, augment your responses with appropriate gestures, such as holding up three fingers, or motioning to three different places, to infuse energy into your response and make your performance more interesting and memorable. (Practice at home so your gestures look natural.) Later, the interviewer will be more likely to recall your three highlights compared to other candidates' laundry lists of information.

By quickly and concisely identifying three areas for each question, you exhibit forethought, analytical skills, and confidence. You will shine and be memorable.

A word of caution: List three strengths, but only one weakness. You want to appear honest and humble, but not crazy.

The Doctor Is In...

"Beware: You can overdo it if you answer every question with the preface 'There are three things I wish to tell you about my qualifications....'"

The following three crazy good examples illustrate how an interviewee can use the "power of three" to his/her advantage.

Example 1

Q. "What skills will you bring to this position?"

A. "I bring three different and distinct skills to this position. The first is my communication skills. The second is my creativity. And the third is my work ethic." Then you would pause and see if the interviewer asks follow-up questions about each skill. If you don't get those follow-up questions, you would proceed to provide examples for each skill.

Example 2

Q. "What are your top strengths?"

A. "I would list the following three areas as my top strengths: extremely versatile, forward thinking, and down to earth." Then as above, add more information to each area.

Example 3

  Q. "What relevant experiences have prepared you for this job?"

  A. "There are three slightly different experiences that have prepared me for this job: one is from a prior position, one is from my current position, and one is from my community volunteer work. Let me address each one with you."

Basically, you take any open-ended question and divide it into three parts. Then, you would discuss and provide examples for each part. You also have the option of saying, "If I could add one more area to my three, it would be . . . ."

Mad About Metaphors

Be cautious about your use of metaphors in a job interview. Metaphors are comparisons between two dissimilar things. Authors use them to make their writing more colorful and easier to understand.

Everyday speech is full of metaphors, such as "it's raining cats and dogs," "I'm going to fix your wagon," "full of piss and vinegar," "the kiss of death," "heart of gold," or "love is a rose."

Metaphors can keep you motivated in your job search in today's tight economy. Think of your job search like a trip to the shopping mall; you try on clothes looking for a good fit and eventually find something worth buying. Or imagine job hunting like a treasure hunt, and you will uncover a gem of a job sooner or later.

When you use metaphors in a job interview, be sure they don't sound too informal or you will come across as unprofessional, as in: "The job was blast" or "My last boss was a real piece of work."

Of course, the interviewers will "get your drift" if you use metaphors to minimize undesirable work situations in your past, such as "the company culture was a prison." Use metaphors sparingly because you should always put a positive spin on previous employment situations.

7 | Your Worldview on Work

What is your *worldview*? The word itself sounds abstract and philosophical, like the lofty topic at a coffee shop debate among bespectacled college professors wearing tweed jackets with suede elbow patches. Not so.

Your worldview is at the foundation of your core values and it has hands-on practicality in your daily life. It is a collection of your convictions, attitudes, and opinions that defines your beliefs about reality. It is the lens through which you see the big picture. It triggers your reactions and responses to the world and to life itself, and it determines your sense of right and wrong.

Here are some examples of worldviews:

- My happiness depends on the happiness of people around me.
- I need to be independent and take charge of my own life.
- It is important for me to excel over those around me.

Your worldview helps you answer thought-provoking questions, such as:

- Who am I?
- Where did I come from?
- What is my purpose in life?

Applying Your Worldview to Work

Instinctively, you use your worldview to make large and small decisions in all areas of your life. You can apply it to your attitudes about work and your career choices. How do you view work? Do you view it as a way to use your talents and skills, make a positive impact on your community or the world, help solve other people's problems, make a difference, or make a living?

Interviewers probably will not use the term worldview, but you will know they are referring to it when they ask the following questions:

- What role does work play in your life?
- How would you describe your ideal job?
- What is a great day at work for you?
- What type of co-workers do you prefer?
- How would you describe your ideal employer?

Work Makes the World Go 'Round

The world is driven by work. It's part of life that consumes an enormous number of waking hours. If you are not lucky enough to be born with a silver spoon in your mouth, win the lottery, marry a millionaire, or rob a bank without getting caught, chances are good that you will work to earn a living.

The workaday world is a recurring theme of many hit songs that celebrate or damn work (okay, mainly damn it) and pay tribute to the 40-hour work week, including:

- *Workin' for a Livin'* by Huey Lewis and the News. The song title about working stiffs says it all. The prospect of never earning enough money or not receiving a well-deserved bonus or salary increase is a common refrain for those who are just scraping by.

- *A Hard Day's Night* by The Beatles. The Fab Four wail about working like dogs. Obviously, this was before they made megabucks and became cultural icons.
- *Working for the Weekend* by Lover Boy. Well, the song title is partly true. Some people work for the weekend, while others work on the weekend, usually in service-oriented industries that cater to people who don't work on weekends.
- *Taking Care of Business* by Bachman–Turner Overdrive. Work is business when you make serious cash. But you still have to bust your tail to "catch your train on time and get to work by nine and start your slaving job to get your pay."
- *9 to 5* by Dolly Parton. Working eight hours a day can be a real grind. Why not five hours? Or three? In the movie *Office Space*, computer geek Peter Gibbons admits he performs only 15 minutes of actual work in any given week. (You call that work? Sounds pretty cushy to me.)
- *Money for Nothing* by Dire Straits. If you learned to play the guitar or drums, you could make money doing nothing on MTV. That beats installing microwave ovens or moving refrigerators and color TVs. "And the chicks are free."
- *She Works Hard for the Money* by Donna Summer. This is a timeless message that motivates women to take charge of their lives. The song, which chronicles a food server's tough times making ends meet, became the "You go, girlfriend" cheer before people said, "You go, girlfriend."
- *Manic Monday* by The Bangles. Everyone dreads Monday, but this song wistfully contrasts a mundane work routine with the joys in life.
- *Draggin' the Line* by Tommy James. The 60s and 70s pop idol sings about working hard (on his farm) and "hugging a tree when you get near it." (Note: The lyrics sparked the term "tree huggers" in reference to people interested in ecology.)
- *The Banana Boat Song (Day-O)* by Harry Belafonte. Dock workers in the Caribbean load bananas onto ships all night long and look forward to going home at sunrise. You can almost smell their gritty sweat.

And let's not forget the American folk classics, *I've Been Working on the Railroad* and *Sixteen Tons*. Hard work built this great country of ours.

Clearly, all of these songs convey a worldview that sees work as drudgery, which could be related to the lyricists' own attitudes about work, or simply because hard work is a staple topic in the music industry. What, then, are some joyful reasons that people work besides earning a paycheck?

- A love for what they do
- Personal fulfillment
- To contribute to the greater good
- To accomplish personal and professional goals
- Camaraderie with coworkers
- To enjoy client interaction
- To fill time with activity
- Change and challenges
- Recognition

The best worldview regarding work is using all of your talents and abilities while you develop and grow as a person and make a difference in the world. Not too many jobs fit this description, but it is something to which you can aspire. Hopefully, you will find employment that allows you to whistle while you work instead of telling your employer to take this job and shove it.

Whatever your personal reasons for working, the bottom line is that almost everyone works for money, compensation, salary, remuneration, or whatever you want to call it. It pays for a roof over your head, clothes on your back, and food in your mouth. It also enables you to take care of your family, send your children to college, buy the latest high-tech gadgets, take vacations, and save for retirement.

Worldview Provides Career Direction

If you desperately need a job and are willing to consider any offer, then your worldview may not make any difference. You need a job, any job, so you can pay your bills. However, having a worldview or philosophy of life might give you some career direction, help you in your job search, and enable you to zero in on what you want in a job. Your worldview will help you avoid jobs that are a poor match for your talents and abilities. As you mature, you can look for a job that aligns with your worldview and philosophy of life as shown in the following three examples.

Home Sweet Home

A candidate hoped to use her architecture/design background to create sustainable housing to address urban decay. Her worldview is that everyone deserves a chance and having a safe and secure home leads to the betterment of society.

Crazy good worldview: People are put on this planet to use their talents and abilities to serve those who are less fortunate.

Crazy bad worldview: People are put on this planet to use their talents and abilities for their own benefit and hedonistic pleasures. Skin on skin; let the love begin.

R-E-S-P-E-C-T

A candidate who believes that everyone should be treated with dignity and respect applied to a medical residency program that operates a free clinic as part of the residency. Residents, faculty, staff, and students work together to impact health care.

Crazy good worldview: Everyone deserves respect, even those who are unemployed and have no insurance. Everyone working together can make a difference.

Crazy bad worldview: Respect yourself. Who cares about anyone else? Every man for himself.

Independence Day

An individual who believes that you get ahead on your own merit and hard work applied for a position based solely on commission. If he does the work, he will be paid well. He is the master of his own destiny and he controls how much he earns based on his own efforts.

Crazy good worldview: You get ahead in life based on your own efforts. Hard work is rewarded.

Crazy bad worldview: You get ahead in life based on your own efforts and sticking it to the man every chance you get.

Mapping a Career Plan

Create a career plan that aligns with your worldview, and pinpoints where you want to be in three, five, and even 10 years. Career planning, in reality, is a lifelong process that involves choosing a career, getting a job, growing in your job, making a possible career change, and, finally, retiring. For purposes of this book, we will concentrate on getting a job.

When you have a plan in hand—or even in your mind—it helps determine your career direction. You might start in an entry-level job to get your foot in the door, and then acquire new skills and certifications, so you can climb the career ladder. In each job you hold, you can determine what you like and don't like about it, the type of people you enjoy working with, and the type of work you like doing. When people job hop with no direction, they may never end up in their ideal job, or they may never know their ideal job.

As Richard N. Bolles, author of the best-selling career guide, *What Color is Your Parachute?* puts it:

> Good career choice or career planning postpones the "narrowing down" until it has first broadened your horizons and expanded the number of options you are thinking about. For example, you're in the newspaper business, but have you ever thought of teaching, or drawing or doing fashion? You first expand your mental horizons, to see all the possibilities, and only then do you start to narrow them down to the particular two or three that interest you the most.

A career plan with a timeline keeps you focused and on track in your job search. It helps you plan ahead and consider many job options. Often, people get their hopes up for just one job. If they do not get it, they become discouraged and may even abandon their job search. If you are open to many options, your ego will not be deflated if one falls through.

Writing down your goals and committing them to paper will raise your spirits and make you feel like you are making some headway. When the interviewer asks about your job search efforts, you can respond positively with, "I posted my resume on several sites. I search online job postings daily, and send letters of inquiry to organizations that could benefit from my skills and talents." These proactive statements show that you are organized, systematic, and persistent, which are good traits to have associated with your candidacy.

Be nimble in your job search. Organize your time, your contacts, and conduct your search thoughtfully according to your career plan. Then, be ready to toss it aside and react to that last-minute call.

Your career timeline should project one to three years out in a down economy. Think about the future and the bigger picture down the road. Ask yourself what types of skills you will need, such as the ability to work with all four generations (Silents, Baby Boomers, Generation X, and Generation Y), communicate effectively, and be tech savvy. You should sign up for courses, seminars, and workshops that will add to your skill sets in hot areas, such as the latest software technology, communications, and conflict resolution.

The Doctor Is In . . .

"Find out if your community offers any free workshops where you can learn and network at the same time."

Many interviewers will inquire about your career goals by asking the following questions:

- How does this job align with your professional development?
- Why are you applying for this job at this point in your career?
- What type of position do you want to be in ultimately?
- If offered this job, what would be your next job after this one?

One of the most frequently asked questions is: Where do you want to be in five years (or three years)? The best way to answer this question is to focus on the job itself and how you would use your skills to accomplish the job duties. "After five years, I hope to assume new responsibilities in a higher position in the organization. Professional development is important to me, and I would like to continually add new skills to my repertoire to enhance my value in the organization."

If you don't have any career goals, or you just haven't thought that far in advance, sell your skill sets. Talk about your hard work ethic and enthusiasm. Describe your hunger to do whatever the job requires, and a willingness to roll up your sleeves. Talk about trying to get your foot in the door and learn the business from the ground up. Do not mention that you need a paycheck to pay your overdue bills, your electricity has just been shut off, and your landlord is ready to evict you for nonpayment of rent—you will come off as a real desperado.

When Job and Worldview Don't Align

If you receive a job offer that does not align with your worldview and career plan, then you have a difficult decision to make. Is a bird in the hand worth two in the bush? Sometimes, yes. If the wolves are howling at the door, and you have a family to feed, then accept the job offer and keep your eyes open for a better job. Sometimes it is easier to get a job when you have a job. You will need to make the decision based on your own unique set of circumstance and the importance of your worldview.

There are some positives to veering off your career course. People from different backgrounds with unique experiences often bring fresh perspectives to a job. In fact, many discoveries in the sciences can be credited to individuals who were newcomers to that particular field. By applying a different viewpoint or set of experiences to a job outside of your comfort zone, you might do something extraordinary.

Some people are risk takers and like to veer off course to add cool new experiences to their worldview. It is a great way to gain a fresh perspective. Most people don't try this, preferring to play it safe.

You must change your career path if your industry is imploding due to the economy or if technology is taking over. Think automotive or manufacturing. Think about what happened to the *Encyclopedia Britannica* when Wikipedia appeared. In addition, look into your crystal ball to see if there could be any external threats to the organization or your job. Try to stay ahead of the curve by adding skills to your unique value proposition (UVP).

Square Peg, Round Hole

How do you respond to an interviewer who observes that the job doesn't match your skills; for example, you are overqualified, or your expertise lies in other areas? He wants to hire you, but thinks you might be unhappy working there.

Emphasize how your experience and skills fit the job, or how they could be adapted. Talk about your transferable skills that are a good match for the job duties. If you are overqualified or your expertise lies in other areas, you could say:

"This job lies slightly out of my past positions, but it fits into my long-term plan of learning about. . . ."

"My qualifications might seem a little more than what is required for this position, but where I think they might be best utilized in this position is in the area of X because I can do the following. . . (list your skill sets)."

The Doctor Is In . . .

"You must be multi-talented, cross-trained, and have adaptable skills in today's marketplace. Just doing your job doesn't cut it anymore. Add as many skills to your repertoire as possible."

PART II

ACT Out: Communicate

8

Bridge the Generational Gap with Crazy Good Behavior

Does age matter? Yes, it really does in an interview. It pays to be aware of your interviewer's generational age. Smart interviewees use their knowledge about each generation to speak the same language and make a favorable impression. This is the first chapter in the Communicate phase of the ACT Out interview strategy, and it explains how members of different generations can communicate effectively with one another.

Defining "Generation"

What is a *generation* anyway? There are several definitions. The first is the offspring in the same stage of descent from a common ancestor; for example, a father and son represent two different generations. Another definition is the average interval between the parents' birth and birth of their offspring. Still another holds that a generation is a group of individuals born and living at the same time who experience the same events.

"A generation is a group of people who share a common location in history and, as a consequence, have a collective persona that not all members share, but they can all relate to," according to historian William Strauss, co-author of *The Fourth Turning*, a landmark book on generational change.

According to this definition, people who were kids when poodle skirts and Elvis Presley became popular belong to one generation. People who were kids when the movie *Grease* debuted and who wore platform shoes and listened to disco music are part of another generation. People who wear sagged pants and listen to rap music belong to still another generation.

Today's multi-generational workplace is composed of four distinct generations vying for jobs.

- The Silent Generation (also called Traditionalists or Veterans), born 1925–1945.
- Baby Boomers (or Boomers or Baby Busters), born 1946–1964.
- Gen X (sometimes called Slackers, which they hate and resent), born 1965–1983.
- Gen Y (also referred to as the Nexters, Millennials, or the ME generation), born 1984–2002.

Each generation has its own unique set of values and way of interviewing. If you know each generation's values and are familiar with some of the world events that occurred during their lifetimes, you can tailor your responses to bridge the generation gap. This term was coined in the 1960s to refer to the differences in values, attitudes, and tastes between one generation and another, particularly parents and their children. The gap occurs when members of different generations do not understand each other because of these differences.

From grumpy old men to the young and restless, it pays to know a little bit about each group so you can adapt your behavior and speak to their values. The following descriptions contain broad statements on observed behaviors that have been measured and analyzed. Be aware that not all statements pertain to all individuals in a generation.

The Sound of "Silents" (Born 1925–1945)

The term Silent Generation—also called "Silents"—first appeared in *Time* magazine's cover story on November 5, 1951, to describe the generation that was coming of age. In their book, *Generations: The History of America's Future, 1584–2069*, authors William Strauss and Neil Howe used this term to describe the generation born 1925–1945. This generation is sandwiched between the war heroes of the G.I. Generation, also called "The Great Generation" (born 1901–1924), and the youthful, free-spirited Baby Boomers (born 1946–1964).

The term "Silent" is not completely accurate. It is true that many Silents are quiet, hardworking people who focused on advancing their careers and conforming to social norms, while coping with American social upheavals, such as the Civil Rights and Women's Lib movements. However, other Silents became outspoken activists, including Martin Luther King, Jr., Gloria Steinem, Malcolm X, Betty Friedan, and Ralph Nader.

Some people hold the theory that people in this generation were dubbed "silent" because they kept their political views to themselves after Senator Joseph McCarthy's anti-communism inquisitions. Other famous Silents include Aretha Franklin, Dustin Hoffman, and Colin Powell.

Historical Events

The oldest Silents are the children of the Great Depression. They lived through the stock market crash of 1929 and experienced its difficult aftermath firsthand. They saw the re-working of the United States under the New Deal of Franklin Delano Roosevelt, which resulted in unemployment rates dropping from 25 percent to 2 percent.

They witnessed how Japan's attack on Pearl Harbor led to the United States' involvement and fighting in World War II. They lived during the post-war economic boom that led to explosive growth and migration to the suburbs. They watched as color television was introduced and became a fixture in the nation's living rooms. In the process, they created the American dream of having a family, owning a home, and getting a great job.

Workplace Profile

Today, Silents are in their sixties, seventies, and eighties, and about 95 percent are retired from the workforce. You'll find them swinging golf clubs on the links, or playing checkers in retirement communities. Employed Silents are eyeballing retirement and counting down their time in the workplace. Unfortunately, some Silents have returned to employment because of current economic conditions. (You have seen them cheerfully greeting customers at the entrance of a major retail chain.)

Silents are experienced workers, who have seen and heard most everything in the workplace, let alone in a job interview. As a generation, they are family-oriented, experienced, reliable (sometimes to a fault), hard working, dedicated, and hold conservative values. They live by a command and control code, and they believe in law and order. They are decreasing in number and they want respect for all that they have done for their country over the years.

"Silent" interviewers place a great deal of importance on hard work, loyalty, and consistency. Your clothes, your demeanor, and your state of mind (mostly your attitude) will be sized up immediately. Old-school values come into play. Right or wrong, this generation believes in working your way up the ladder, putting in your time on a consistent basis, and being loyal to your employer and fellow workers. Silents are good team players who don't like to ruffle any feathers or initiate conflict in the workplace.

Civility also seems to be on the minds of Silents as they turn their organizations over to new leaders and emerging workers. They do not believe in rudeness, dropping F-bombs in conversations, or showing a lack of manners. Do not even think about answering your cell phone or texting when you are conversing with them. That is the fastest way to reduce your chances of getting hired.

To make a favorable impression, exhibit the following crazy good behaviors when interviewing with someone from the Silent generation:

- Use a strong, but not a crushing, handshake.
- Make strong eye contact and smile slightly upon being introduced.
- Talk politely and be respectful.
- Enunciate clearly.
- Use appropriate words, and avoid slang and jargon.

- Emphasize areas where you have displayed loyalty.
- Show examples of your commitment to previous jobs.
- Be honest about your job experience and qualifications.
- Listen to each question completely before jumping in with your answer.

Rate the Behavior

Using the Psychotron, how would you rate the following interviewer's behavior?

A Piercing Noise

At a medical school workshop on interviewing, a senior faculty member asked me if his school could, by law, limit an applicant's number of body piercings.

"By law," I said, "No, you can't."

This did not go over very well with this faculty member who then went off on a shrill rant about the younger generation. "They have no respect for traditions and the way we have done things for years. They think they can dress however they want. They pierce their bodies, and even their tongues. Patients are so turned off by that. And don't get me started on their work ethic, if you can even call it that. What is the world coming to?" On and on it went until he finally wound down.

I pitied the next medical school applicant who arrived dressed even slightly inappropriately and, God forbid, with any visible piercings.

Did the faculty member exhibit crazy good behavior by sticking to his conservative values, or was it crazy bad because he showed that he was rigid and intolerant of the younger generation? How would you handle this situation if you were the applicant, and you had a body piercing?

The Doctor Is In . . .

"Silents have seen a lot in their day. Don't be afraid to dream big and to express those dreams as part of your interview. This generation set the American values. The more you reference them, the more likely you can connect with them."

Big, Bad Baby Boomers (Born 1946–1964)

The term baby boom identifies the enormous increase in births in the United States following World War II, and its resultant Baby Boomers. In Canada, they are called Boomies. Britain refers to them as the Bulge. The first baby boomers reached the retirement age of 65 in 2011.

Many of your interviewers will be Baby Boomers. They were reared on television, and are the products of *I Love Lucy, Captain Kangaroo, Lassie,* and my personal favorite, *Leave It to Beaver.* (Everyone remembers June constantly asking Ward Cleaver not to be so rough on the Beaver.) They took family trips with Mom *and* Dad before the invention of the minivan, and rode in the back of a wood-paneled station wagon facing the cars behind them.

If the Silent generation created the American Dream, then the Baby Boomer generation is living it. They grew up in the post-war boom and rebelled against their parents and authority (only to find themselves in positions of power today). As a generation, they see themselves as hardworking, educated, competitive, loyal, ambitious, and idealistic. Silent parents wanted their Baby Boomer offspring to succeed them and surpass what they had achieved. For the most part, the Boomers have done so.

Oprah Winfrey, Donald Trump, Bill Gates, Bill Clinton, and George W. Bush are famous Baby Boomers.

Historical Events

Baby Boomers saw the Russians launch Sputnik and experienced the space race, as well as the cold war. In school, they practiced duck and cover drills, in preparation for a Soviet missile attack, and they watched their neighbors build bomb shelters in their back yards. The assassination of John

F. Kennedy ended Camelot, followed by the killings of Martin Luther King, Jr., and Bobby Kennedy.

The Beatles arrived and forever changed music for their generation (and for subsequent ones, too). Woodstock would follow. The Boomers burned bras, resisted the draft, witnessed violent protests, and watched as the Vietnam War tore at the country. The Kent State massacre only added to the divide within the country. Watergate cemented their disillusionment and poor opinion of politics and government.

Workplace Profile

Baby Boomers believe that hard work will pay off, often over talent and brains. They work hard and party harder. Many Baby Boomers are in or are moving into leadership positions within their organizations, both at the senior- and mid-management levels. Given the current economy, many of them, however, are staying in their jobs longer because their retirement plans took a major hit. As their hair has grayed over the years, they have created a gray ceiling by staying in the workforce longer than usual. They would like to retire, but they are worried that they might run out of money. So they remain employed even though they are sick and tired of being re-organized, re-engineered, and re-configured. This has created somewhat of a logjam for the younger generations in the hiring process.

The important thing to know is that Boomers believe you get ahead in life through hard work and education. They believe you have to pay your dues. They place a huge amount of importance on earning their respect; it will not be given to you freely.

To make a favorable impression, exhibit the following crazy good behaviors when interviewing with someone from the Baby Boomer generation:

- Show your willingness to work hard and do whatever it takes to get a job done.
- Indicate that you are willing to pay your dues and learn the ropes of the job.
- Emphasize how you have improved upon or increased your education, and you are a life-long learner.
- Avoid any hint of entitlement. This generation can't stand that fragrance.

- Be willing to share how you create balance in your life. It is appropriate to talk about your hobbies and interests outside of work.
- Share your ambition and dreams. Detail your goals and how you are going to accomplish them.
- Demonstrate your knowledge of what they have accomplished, and how you might be able to build on that with their guidance.
- Show respect, which is equally important to this generation as it is to the Silent generation.
- Understand that Boomers think that they are the epitome of cool, so go along with it. They recognize they are aging, but don't want other people to notice it, as shown in the following past and present list of trends.

Baby Boomers, Then and Now:

- Then: Muscle cars
- Now: Muscle cramps
- Then: Red hot mama
- Now: Red hot flashes
- Then: *You're So Vain*
- Now: Varicose veins
- Then: Full of piss and vinegar
- Now: Full of piss and Viagra
- Then: Pot of gold (weed)
- Now: Pot of gold (bed pan)
- Then: The Rolling Stones
- Now: Kidney Stones
- Then: Bo Derek
- Now: BoTox

Rate the Behavior

Using the Psychotron, how would you rate this job hunter's behavior?

Old and New

Mark had taken an early retirement and was all set to live the good life, especially after working his tail off and paying his dues.

As the economy continued its downward spiral, he realized that he would have to return to the workforce. But who was going to hire someone approaching 60, and who had been out of work for seven years?

Using traditional job-hunting methods, Mark updated his resume and wondered how he would handle the seven-year employment lapse. He decided to gloss over those years. He printed 100 resumes and started sending them out to various companies in his previous industry. Nothing came back. Zero. Zip. Zilch.

As he neared the end of his stack of resumes, he finally realized that he would have to change his strategy to get an interview, at least a screening interview. So, he went online and rebuilt his resume, adding a new set of skills from the past seven years.

When Mark started receiving responses, his biggest surprise was learning the screening interviews would be conducted by phone. There would be no face-to-face contact, and he would have to sell himself over the phone. It was, in his words, horrible at first.

Luckily, he picked up some tricks. He stood up and moved around when he wanted to inject some energy into his voice. He used a wireless headset, which allowed him to gesture, even though he knew the person on the other end couldn't see him. He tacked notes up on the wall about the skills and competencies that he wanted to emphasize. Finally, he talked about what he had learned during the past seven years, especially about planning and adjusting when his plans didn't pan out, being flexible, and still having the energy to work.

Did Mark exhibit crazy good behavior for abandoning his old ways to find a job, or was it crazy bad behavior because he wandered into the uncharted territory of the online world?

Real-life result: Mark aced his phone interview and advanced to a face-to-face interview, which he nailed. He was offered the position, partially because of his old style of working in a new world.

The Doctor Is In . . .

"Silents and Baby Boomers will be most impressed in an interview by examples of your hard work and your willingness to pay your dues. Show respect for what they have accomplished and how you can build upon their work."

The Internet Generation X (Born 1965–1983)

The term Gen X was coined by British writer Jane Deverson in 1964 to describe a particular group of young people who did not accept traditional social mores. The term was later popularized in Douglas Coupland's groundbreaking novel, *Generation X: Tales for an Accelerated Culture*. Hugh Jackman, Halle Berry, Jennifer Lopez, Dr. Dré, Robert Downey, Jr., and Mary Lou Retton are famous Gen Xers.

Gen X grew up during a time of massive change within the family dynamics. Both parents typically worked as they tried to achieve the American Dream. As their parents were busy with their careers, Gen Xers were sent to after-school activities and were labeled latch key kids.

They grew up with divorced parents, Minivans, and soccer moms. Personal computers were in their homes and bedrooms. MTV ruled. During all of this, they experienced times of great uncertainty.

Historical Events

This generation saw the first *Star Wars* movie released, they experienced the Iranian Crisis, and they saw Ronald Reagan elected President of the United States. They awoke in the wee hours to watch Prince Charles marry Diana. They watched transfixed and saddened as the Space Shuttle Challenger exploded upon liftoff, killing all seven astronauts aboard.

The fall of the Berlin Wall occurred during their formative years. The Los Angeles Race Riots grabbed their attention on TV, and they spent a summer afternoon watching a white Bronco on the freeways of LA and wondered how it would end.

Workplace Profile

Gen X initially appeared bored, aimless, and disrespectful, thus, earning the tag of slackers. As stated earlier, they don't care for this term and with good reason: They have demonstrated a strong and successful entrepreneurial spirit. They are moving into positions of leadership and will be pushing the Baby Boomers out on a daily basis. In fact, slacker successes are as plentiful as websites. Business journals dubbed them the "Entrepreneurial Generation," and featured rags-to-riches profiles on Jerry Yang, the multibillionaire co-founder of Yahoo!, and Sky Dayton, the multimillionaire behind Earthlink. Not all Gen Xers are getting rich, but most of them have stopped playing video games, gotten off the sofa, and are searching for their place in the world.

Some important things to know about Gen X are that they believe in creating balance in their lives, they are family-focused, and they are street- and tech-savvy. They are also passionate (especially once they have found their passion), creative, and social in nature.

To make a favorable impression, you should exhibit the following crazy good behaviors when interviewing with a Gen Xer:

- Demonstrate that you understand the expectations of the workplace and the various jobs you have had.
- Share examples of your creativity.
- Show how you accomplish tasks in a timely fashion.
- Provide specific instances when you employed independent thinking.
- Praise the work of former colleagues and co-workers.
- Indicate how work/life balance makes you better professionally and personally.
- Highlight your efficiency in your work.

Rate the Behavior

Using the Psychotron, how would you rate the job candidate's behavior in the following real-life interview?

The Inquisition

Patricia arrived early for her interview and was ushered into a small conference room. Before the interviewer opened his mouth, Patricia politely inquired if she could ask some questions to learn more about the position. The interviewer thought that this might prove interesting, so he said yes. However, he was speechless when she asked the following presumptuous questions:

- How much vacation time do I get in the first year, and when does it increase?
- Will I get my own personal laptop?
- Will the company pay for my home cable and Internet service?
- Do you have onsite daycare?
- When can I expect my first bonus?

Did Patricia exhibit crazy good behavior by obtaining important job-related information upfront, or was it crazy bad behavior because she put the proverbial cart before the horse?

Real-life result: Needless to say, Patricia did not get the job, although the interviewer did have some fun as he explored with her in greater detail why she wanted to know about this information before even talking about the position and her qualifications.

The Doctor Is In . . .

"Gen Xers are emerging into leadership roles. They want to do things differently. Show how you will fit into those plans. Use concrete examples to illustrate how you have implemented your creative ideas."

High-Tech Generation Y (Born 1984–2002)

Generation Y combines the can-do attitude of Silents, the teamwork of Boomers, and the high-tech know-how of Generation X. Gen Y exceeds the Baby Boomer generation in size, and it comprises a quarter of the U.S. population.

Interestingly, Gen Y has a lot in common with Boomers and has been called the echo-boom. They share their Baby Boomer parents' overwhelming desire to succeed. Gen Y grew up in a very structured, busy, and over planned world because their parents worked long hours and signed them up for classes, sports, and other after-school activities.

Gen Y displays tremendous curiosity and is forever asking why, as in these questions:

- Y should I do household chores?
- Y should I find a job when my parents will support me?
- Y should I find an apartment when I can live at home?
- Y should I purchase my own car?

They cut their teeth on The Learning Channel and Peter Piper Pizza. This generation's members know more about digital technology than their parents or teachers. Today's university graduates, for example, have never experienced a world without cell phones, DVD players, pixel-rich screen displays, and instantaneous, soundless wireless access. There have always been computers, the Internet, and they have no clue how to use a typewriter. Chances are good that they've changed IP providers more than they've changed schools. With iPods, iPhones and Droids, YouTube, Skype, Facebook, and Twitter, everything is quick and flashy. If it is on the Internet, it must be true

Famous Gen Ys include Christina Aguilera, Venus Williams, Princes William and Harry, Michael Phelps, and Lindsay Lohan.

Historical Events

If Gen X grew up thinking that the world was changing around them, Gen Y was born already knowing it. Constant change, at lightning speeds, is the norm. They have grown up knowing that history is no longer just the purview of textbooks, but it can happen in a moment's notice. Natural disaster, violent events, war, and major technological advances have played a huge role for this generation.

There was the malfunction at Three Mile Island nuclear power plant, which caused a near meltdown, and the Exxon Valdez, which spilled more than ten million gallons of oil into Prince William Sound. There was the Waco Siege by the FBI and ATF on the David Koresh's Branch Davidian compound. They witnessed the Oklahoma City and Olympic (Atlanta) bombings. They saw the Columbine High School shootings leave 13 students and one teacher dead and the campus shootings at Northern Illinois and Virginia Tech. Of course, this generation experienced September 11, when U.S. planes were hijacked in attacks on the World Trade Center and the Pentagon, killing more than 3,000 people, and leading to the country's ongoing war against terrorism. They watched natural disasters, such as Hurricane Katrina and the Tsunami in the Indian Ocean.

On a high note, they saw the first African-American U.S. President elected and shared in the excitement of releases of the bestselling Harry Potter series and *Twilight*, which sparked vampire-mania.

Workplace Profile

Gen Y is living in a time when everything is pretty much instantaneous due to rapidly advancing technology. There are three important things to know about this generation:

1. They live and breathe technology.
2. They have strong self-awareness.
3. They have short-attention spans because of their media consuming habits. They send and read news updates in 140 characters or less.

To make a favorable impression, you should exhibit the following crazy good behaviors when interviewing with someone from Generation Y:

- Don't assume that because of their relatively young age that they are not in roles of leadership.

- Recognize that your personal goals are important to them.
- Use technology to make your point or to showcase your talents.
- Gen Y is visual, so bring samples or info-graphics to illustrate your accomplishments.
- Let your Gen Y interviewer know you can multi-task and shift from one project to another quickly and easily.
- Gen Y encourages people to seek a well-paying, enjoyable job.
- Optimism is highly valued.
- Loyalty is important, but it is not highly valued because many of this generation change jobs frequently.
- Share your career plan during the interview.
- Do not be informal with Gen Yers, just because they are young.

Rate the Behavior

Using the Psychotron, how would you rate the mother's job-hunting advice to her teen-age daughter in the following real-life anecdote?

Mother Knows Best

A colleague shared her experience with her teenage daughter's job hunt. Her mission statement probably would read: *"I want a fun job that makes me happy."* Teenagers are guided by the unrealistic assumption that everyone who's hiring will welcome them with open arms.

"Being a veteran parent, on child number three, I finally got the hang of advising first time job seekers in the modern culture. I told my daughter she would not be driving a c-a-r unless she had a j-o-b.

I encouraged her to apply for every 'fun' job she could find. Next, I advised her to create a resume if for no other reason than have a cheat sheet at hand when talking to potential employers.

So, we set out to begrudgingly build her resume, which would, of course, be light in content. We talked about design and how she could say something about herself without really having a job history. We perused other resumes and generated some ideas for hers.

Finally, off she went with her 'stupid' resume in hand. Imagine her disillusionment when she discovered that hiring managers were not cheering as she filled out job applications.

Imagine my smug expression when she returned from her on-the-spot interviews at the pizza joint, the grocery store, and the mall with glowing remarks from prospective employers on how she was able to relate her life experiences listed on her resume to the job requirements.

She didn't get every job she applied for, nor did she even get a 'fun' job. But she did get a job.

Now she is starting a job that she really wants at a medical center, working with special needs kids after school and during summer camps. She wouldn't have gotten that job without previous work experience.''

Mom's insistence that her daughter create a resume was a crazy good job-hunting strategy after all.

The Doctor Is In . . .

"Be cautious about assuming the age of your interviewer. With a little practice, though, you can hone in on the values that each generation holds most dear. You can shape your answer using the language of their values."

9 | Types of Interviews

Interviews have come a long way since traditional one-on-one meetings at the employer's place of business. With the advent of technology, the interview process might be conducted by phone, Skype, or in a one-on-one, panel, group interview, or any combination thereof. Smart job seekers will become proficient at all of these interview methods.

Phone Interviews: Can You Hear Me Now?

In today's job market, it's important to know how to give good phone . . . and no, this is not in reference to the 800 numbers that are advertised on late-night TV. Employers use phone interviews as a time-saving, cost-efficient method for screening job applicants and eliminating candidates whose skills and job experience do not match the job requirements. Phone interviews are designed to screen candidates and winnow the pool of applicants who will be invited for in-person interviews.

Phone interviews are conducted just like in-person interviews. Often, they are used to save on the traditional travel and hotel expenses involved in interviewing candidates who reside out of town or out of state. While you're actively job searching, it's important to be prepared for a phone interview on a moment's notice. You never know when a human resources manager, headhunter, or a networking contact might call. Most of the time, however, you will receive a call to schedule a phone interview appointment about a job opening.

No matter how or where your interview is conducted, your goal is to communicate that you are the best candidate for the position. If the interview has been scheduled in advance, you should prepare as carefully as you would for a formal, sit-down, face-to-face in someone's office. Do not underestimate the importance of a phone interview. It is critical to use proper etiquette to make a good impression on the interviewer, so you can progress to the next stage of the interview process.

You're probably wondering, "How hard can a phone interview be? I talk on the phone every day." True, but most of the time, you don't have a potential job offer at stake, and the listener is not sitting with a checklist in hand scrutinizing your every word. You will be graded on your enthusiasm, clarity, politeness, and the types of questions you ask. You will need to clean up your grammar, avoid run-on sentences, and padding, such as "er," "um," "uh," and "you know." Keep in mind that the interview process is a two-way street (a polite street with traffic rules), and you should be checking out the interviewer, who is a representative of the employer organization. You may not want to accept every job offer that comes your way.

The interesting news is that practice makes habit; so practice perfectly. You should prepare for a phone interview in many of the same ways you would prepare for a face-to-face interview, such as practicing your responses to a list of common interview questions about your education, professional background, your strengths, and your weaknesses. It wouldn't hurt to have a recording device handy so you can hear how you sound when you conduct a mock interview with a family member or a friend. As the old adage goes, "Success comes when opportunity meets preparation."

It is useful to have your resume and notes close at hand, so you can refer to them quickly and quietly when you formulate your responses to the interviewer's questions.

- Who was your last employer?
- What was your job title?
- What were your dates of employment?
- What were your job responsibilities?
- Why did you leave?
- What are your salary expectations?
- What interests you in this job?
- Why do you think you are qualified to do this job?
- Why do you want to work for this company?
- Do you have any questions about the job or the company?
- Are you willing to travel?
- What is your greatest strength?
- What is your greatest weakness?
- How well to you handle stress on the job?
- Are you able to meet deadlines?
- What are your career goals?
- What is your ideal work environment?

At the end of the interview, the employer will usually ask if the job candidate has any questions about the job or the organization. Warning: Under no circumstances should you say that you have no questions. Employers will judge you based on your questions. If you don't have three to five thoughtful, open-ended questions prepared, you will be viewed as lazy, ill-prepared, unmotivated, or simply not interested.

Your questions should correspond with the stage of the interview process. In the case of a first phone interview, you can get away with asking basic questions, but don't ask about anything that can be found easily on the organization's website. It will look like you haven't done your homework. Before the interview, you should peruse the website and notice if the employer is a company, a corporation, an agency, an association, or some other entity, to ensure that you use the correct terminology. In addition, check out the "Newsroom" tab, or a similarly named tab, that houses press releases on recent product launches, achievements, awards, and other noteworthy news. The more informed you are about your potential employer, the better.

Sample 1:

Crazy good: "I read a press release about the association's monthly magazine winning awards for General Excellence in a high-profile national competition. How do you encourage employees to get involved with organizations that run these types of competitions?"

   Crazy bad: "Do you publish a monthly magazine?"

Sample 2:

Crazy good: "In what ways has the organization recently demonstrated its appreciation of high-performing employees?"

   Crazy bad: "Does your organization pay spot bonuses for showing up on time?"

These questions are appropriate for the initial phone interview.

- What is your organizational structure?
- How do employees communicate with one another to carry out their work?
- How will my leadership responsibilities and performance be measured, and by whom?
- What are the job's day-to-day responsibilities?
- What is the company's management style and what kind of employee fits well with it?
- What are some of the skills and abilities necessary for someone to succeed in this job?

- What is the company policy on professional development, such as workshops, seminars, and classes?
- What particular computer equipment and software do you use?
- How frequently are formal and informal reviews given to new employees?
- How much guidance or assistance is made available to individuals in developing career goals?

The Doctor Is In . . .

"For a phone interview, stand up to add energy to your conversation. You don't have to be sitting for the entire interview. Move around to pump up your energy level. Scotch tape any notes to the wall so you can read them at eye level. Remember that when you smile, listeners can hear it in your voice."

Before the Interview: Ready and Waiting

- Designate a quiet area where you can talk on the phone undisturbed with no distractions. Translation: Order your kids out of the room. (Better yet, tell them to play outside or go to a friend's house.) Turn off the TV and background music. Let the dog out in the backyard.
- Turn off the call-waiting mode on your phone, so your interview will not be interrupted by an intermittent beep indicating that a call is waiting. The beep is annoying and distracting. Now is the time to focus on the interview.
- Keep your resume and a list of your accomplishments at your fingertips.
- Prepare a list of questions that you can ask about the job and the company.
- Make sure you have a pen and paper handy, just in case you need to jot down notes or some important contact information.
- Fill a water glass in case your throat feels dry or scratchy during the interview.

During the Interview

- Dress up. Some people swear that wearing business attire for the phone interview will motivate them psychologically to communicate more professionally with the interviewer.
- Speak slowly, modulate your voice, and enunciate clearly. During a phone interview, you must rely on your voice to express your personality, eagerness, and enthusiasm.
- Give succinct answers. If you ramble, the interviewer will zone out.
- Do not interrupt. It is just plain rude.
- If you don't have an immediate response to a question, tell the interviewer you need a moment to think about it.
- Do not chew or slurp while you are talking on the phone. This is unacceptable phone etiquette.

Skype: Smile for the Camera!

Video interviewing has moved into the mainstream for business meetings and job interviews. Many employers are jumping on the Skype video bandwagon to conduct face-to-face interviews because it is a cost-effective way to see the candidate interact with new technology, express themselves on video (an increasingly important task today), and deal with a complex situation.

What exactly is the scoop on Skype?

In May 2011, Microsoft purchased Skype for $8.5 billion. As of September 2011, there were 663 million registered users, and usage is growing by leaps and bounds.

Translation: Get familiar with Skype or get left behind. Skype is a free download. You will need an eyeball camera if your computer does not have a camera built into it. You'll impress potential employers by knowing how to use Skype, or even being brave enough to suggest it yourself.

By becoming comfortable with using Skype, you will be better able to showcase your cyberspace personality or *cyber*personality. Be sure to use your most enthusiastic voice, practically bursting with enthusiasm, and keep smiling. The goal is make your *cyber*personality shine through during the question-and-answer drill and stand out from other candidates who are being asked the same questions.

Your Skype Checklist

1. *Choose a professional username.* You will have more credibility if your Skype account moniker is not meetthegirls42 or thebigguyXX. Ditto for Hotmamma36D or Studmuffin007.

2. *Know Skype inside and out.* Download the software well in advance of the interview. Before your Skype interview, do some practice runs with your friends to become familiar with the technologies and the special features, such as being able to share your screen with the interviewer. This feature allows you to showcase your original graphic designs or your in-progress app or something else.

3. *Check your Internet connection.* Low signal strength will throw a wrench into your interview. Conduct a quick test the morning of the interview to make sure the camera and the microphone are working correctly. If you're using the webcam on your smart phone, make sure you have the battery charged and know exactly where to sit the phone so it captures you and your environment in a flattering manner.

4. *Plug in securely.* Plug your computer into an Ethernet port, and plug your headphones into the computer's jack. You want direct Ethernet access because it's far more stable than wireless, and you want to have headphones in to avoid playback from the speakers

5. *Now hear this!* Looking polished and professional doesn't matter if the interviewer can't hear you. Buy a USB-headset because the microphone jack usually provides a suboptimal experience. Make sure you have working microphones and headphones, if necessary. Test your incoming and outgoing audio before the interview.

6. *Call for backup.* If your main computer crashes, it's a good idea to have another computer on standby. Get your interviewer's phone number and email in case there is a technical emergency (e.g., Internet access or camera doesn't work). This also shows your prospective employer that you plan ahead and are prepared for emergencies.

7. *Set the stage.* A neat, uncluttered backdrop suggests that you are an organized individual, even if you are more of an Oscar than a Felix. The background will be visible during your interview, so opt for a neutral backdrop or bookshelves filled with your favorite volumes. If you're a hoarder or you collect beer cans or heads of wild game, you will need to clean up your mess, move your beloved collectibles, or consider another location that has no unsightly visible distractions for the interview.

8. *Present yourself in a favorable light.* A light behind you, such as daylight streaming through a window or an electric lamp, will make your face look dark on the screen. Place a lamp in front of you to light up your face (halogen lamps often work well), or two task lights on either side of the computer/webcam.

9. *Put a sock in it.* Eliminate all distractions. Turn off your cell phone, TV, and music, and banish your family and pets from the immediate area. Get Fido out of barking range. Some things are out of your control—such as a jet flying overhead or sirens from a fire truck or an ambulance—but you can learn to deal with them coolly and calmly.

10. *Turn off your pop-ups and email.* They slow down your computer a bit and they may distract you from the interview.

11. *Head and shoulders.* If you are sitting too close to the monitor, your mug—no matter how adorable—will fill the entire screen. (And if you have a face that only a mother could love, you might look downright frightening to an interviewer.) Move back, so your shoulders and your shirt show, too, along with your hands on the desktop.

12. *The eyes have it.* Alternate your gaze between the webcam and your computer monitor. If you look only at the webcam, it will seem that you are always looking down. By looking up at the screen occasionally, you will appear more confident and savvy.

13. *Sitting pretty.* By sitting straight and erect, you will look more professional, alert, responsive . . . and slimmer. Picture the newscasters on the nightly news. They always sit tall, yet appear very comfortable and self-assured in front of the camera.

14. *Organize your notes in front of you.* The interviewer cannot see your entire desktop, so use the space wisely to place information that will be helpful to you in responding to questions.

15. *Dress for success.* Contrary to popular belief, "shirt required, pants optional" is not proper Skype interview attire. If you unexpectedly need to stand up, you will need to cover your butt—literally. This is a job interview, so dress as you would for a formal, sit-down, face-to-face interview. Tank tops and board shorts should remain in your beach bag.

Also, keep your striped and houndstooth-patterned shirts tucked away in your closet. They will create visual disturbances when viewed on the webcam. Don't wear white, either, because you will look washed out. Stick to darker colors (gray, navy blue, purple) and add a jewel-tone accent in a tie or a scarf.

FaceTime

FaceTime is Apple's version of Skype. You can use FaceTime as you would Skype. You just need an Apple computer, iPad or iPhone. All of the same rules and suggestions apply. One additional suggestion if you are using your iPhone: Set your phone on a surface that will hold your phone in place so you can move your hands.

One-on-One Interview: Up Close and Personal

Congratulations. You have passed the company's screening process—typically a phone or a Skype (or FaceTime) interview—and you have been asked to come in for a one-on-one interview. The company is already reasonably assured that your skills and experience meet the job requirements. Many people look great on paper and are all that while others don't quite measure up in person. Adam Craft experienced both scenarios with two job candidates who were vying for one position.

Craft is Regional Marketing Director for a company specializing in water damage restoration that frequently posts job openings on Craigslist. He is constantly flooded with e-mails and resume attachments and has found the screening process to be time-consuming. Recently, Craft began asking applicants to include snippets about themselves—unrelated to the position—and why he should contact them.

He says this system weans out people who cannot follow directions and just haphazardly attach a resume. It also expedites the interview and makes it easier to connect with interviewees. Craft says a resume alone rarely gets someone an interview, and he will only interview applicants who exhibit personality and social intelligence.

Below are two e-mail responses from recent applicants (#1 is a male, #2 is a female) who were selected to interview for a Marketing Account

Executive position. Their email responses showed personality, and Craft knew he would hit it off with them.

Craft looks for all the standard signs during the interview: Was the candidate punctual? Did he or she dress the part? Does his or her previous experience outshine other candidates? The true test is if candidates accurately represent themselves in their initial emails and prove they are worth the time investment in a face-to-face meeting.

The two selected candidates responded to this job posting on Craigslist:

We are looking for a Marketing Account Rep to help maintain, solidify, and grow accounts throughout the Dallas-Fort Worth metroplex. Must be able to connect and develop lasting relationships with blue-collar small business owners. We work in the construction field, so this is a not a suit-and-tie type of job. This position is not for a sales guru, but more of an honest and competent relationship builder.

We need someone who is likable, presentable, professional, organized, analytical, and tech savvy. Must be willing to start early and work late as needed. We are a relatively small company that is growing rapidly, and every person plays a significant role in our growth. We do not have time to give someone 12 months to mature into the position.

Candidate must have a clean background, clean driving record, and a valid driver's license as the position involves driving a company vehicle during business hours.

Preferred education: Four-year bachelor's degree

Candidate #1: The Renaissance Man

"Why you will want to call me: I am a Renaissance man or a jack-of-all-trades, identified easily by my thirst for knowledge and expertise in vastly different interests, and my curiosity has always accelerated me toward great things. I have learned much: from building houses to playing the piano, from joining the Army to publishing haikus, from getting my master's degree in business to performing standup comedy. Eventually, I plan to take all of this knowledge and win Jeopardy and climb Mount Everest, but until that day comes, I will keep aspiring for more.

"So why should you call me? True Renaissance men are a rapidly dying breed, and you shouldn't hesitate to utilize me for your own company's profitability.

"I would like to thank you for this opportunity to articulate something about myself for a potential position. It is impossible for a resume and cover letter to fully present one's self. Of course, I have attached these items and hope you see, as I do, the excellent potential and reasons for continuing this conversation."

Candidate #2: The Comic

"To whom it may concern: Your job search ends here. I'm smart, I learn quickly, and I could befriend a wall. Attached is my awesome resume. (Hold on to your socks, because they will surely be knocked off when you read it). I have also attached a picture to prove I'm a real person (but I understand if you make your own silent judgments)."

When asked why he selected these two applicants, Craft said, "The Renaissance man spoke well on the phone and showed a genuine interest in learning and growing. The comic also spoke well and was absolutely hilarious. She kept me laughing the whole time, so I asked her to come in for an interview as soon as possible."

Real-life result: "I hired the Renaissance man because he was experienced, had a strong educational background, and I thought he would help the business grow. His interpersonal skills would enable him to represent the company well to our clients. He also seemed sincere and genuine during the entire interview process.

"Although the comic was hilarious on the phone, she bombed in the interview. I would compare it to the kind of awkward comedy that is sometimes fun to watch on TV but is not-so-fun to witness firsthand. I was tempted to offer a second interview to see if her poor performance was a fluke, but her experience and education were not as impressive as the other candidate's."

It's Showtime!

Hiring processes vary among companies, but you can count on engaging in at least one face-to-face interview. In this traditional format, you will sit down with one company representative, typically a human resources professional, your potential supervisor, or a co-worker to discuss your qualifications in depth and how you would be an asset to the company.

You will have to prove that—above all other candidates—you are the one the company should hire for the position. Use this precious time to establish a good rapport and a personal connection with the interviewer. One of the interviewer's goals is to determine if your personality is a good fit for the organization, the culture, and if you will get along with other employees. If the interviewer takes a liking to you, then you are halfway there.

In a one-on-one, the interviewer will ask you about your past job experiences listed on your resume. Be prepared to answer "Tell me about yourself" by pulling your unique value proposition (UVP) out of your hip pocket. Refer to Chapter 6, which explains UVPs in depth.

You may be asked, "Why would you be a good fit for this job?" Reiterate how your skills align with the job description. Develop in-depth stories based on core elements you heard from the beginning of the application and interview process. For example, if the company is looking for a technology-focused executive, tell an anecdote about your social-media savvy. If the company needs a strategic planner, prepare an anecdote about developing and implementing a strategic plan for a past employer. In the interviewing competition, anecdotes will help you make your point. They will make your interviewers remember you in a sea of bland candidates.

Often, job seekers are so desperate for a job offer that they forget the interview is a two-way street. You are providing your education, talents, job experience, skills, and know-how in exchange for a compensation and benefits package. You should be a discerning shopper because, after all, you have a lot to offer. Read job postings carefully to weed out the time wasters. Job ad jargon could disguise the real story behind some jobs that seem promising on paper. If any of the following phrases appear in the job posting or job description, ask the interviewer for clarification to determine if the opportunity is "crazy good" or "crazy bad."

If the job ad states:	It could mean:
Join our fast-paced company	We have no time to train you. Heck, we can't handle our own jobs.
Duties will vary	You will expected to do everything from shipping packages to taking out the garbage.
Problem-solving skills required	Do you have any experience fixing copy machines?
Requires leadership ability	Someone needs to herd the sheep around here.
Good communication skills	When you figure out what management wants, can you please tell the rest of us?
Must be deadline oriented.	Better hustle. No one has touched your workload in two months.

In your one-on-one interview with an HR professional, you will be asked questions based on your resume. Be specific and follow up each response with an anecdote. It's not enough to say, "I take pride in my work." To shrewd HR managers, this could mean "I blame others for my mistakes." They have heard it all before and cannot be snowed by a clever turn of phrase. If you don't elaborate on this type of general statement immediately, you will be asked to provide an example that supports your claim.

If the applicant says:	It could mean:
I'm an expert at office organization.	I organize the office football pool.
I'm hard-working and dependable.	But I might not always be working on what you want.
I have a wealth of job experience.	I've had plenty of McJobs.
I'm personable.	I like to gossip with my co-workers.
I'm adaptable.	I'm a job hopper.
I'm always on the go.	I'm always going out for lunch or shopping.
I'm very professional.	Check out my iPhone and iPad.

As the HR manager peruses your resume, he or she may notice some lapses in your employment history and question you about them. Do not be ashamed or embarrassed if a previous employer dismissed you from a job. Just chalk it up to experience and a lesson learned that will help you in your future employment.

If the interviewer asks you point-blank about the reason you were let go, you can soften the impact by responding that the company was downsizing its workforce due to economic reasons, or your job function was eliminated due to technology.

Play Nice

It almost goes without saying that you must be on your best behavior in any type of interview to present a professional image and make a favorable impression. Keep your responses to the interviewer's questions focused on the job, how you can benefit the company, and your previous job experience and skills. Do not get chummy with the interviewer or take liberties in making tactless remarks or observations that you find amusing, no matter how comfortable you may feel in the interview setting. For example, do not point and laugh hysterically at family photos on the interviewer's desk. This type of crazy bad behavior will reduce your chances of getting asked back for another interview. Finally, under no circumstances should you comment on the interviewer's appearance, as illustrated in this anecdote that has appeared without attribution on numerous websites, and I can take absolutely no credit for:

All Ears

A man was injured in a serious accident. Fortunately, the only permanent damage he suffered was the amputation of both ears. Due to this unusual handicap, he was self-conscious about his appearance.

As a result of the accident, he received a large sum of money from the insurance company. He decided to fulfill a lifelong dream of owning his own business by purchasing a small, but expanding, computer firm with his settlement. He quickly set out to hire someone who could help him run the business, and he scheduled interviews with his top three candidates.

The first interview went well. The candidate was pleasant and seemed to be very business savvy. At the end of the interview, the man with no ears asked him, "Do you notice anything unusual about me?" The candidate responded, "You don't have any ears." This made him angry and he threw the first candidate out.

The second interview went even better than the first. At the end of the interview, the man with no ears asked, "Do you notice anything unusual about me?" The second candidate replied, "You have no ears." Again, the man became infuriated and threw the second candidate out.

The third and final interview was the best of all three. Feeling certain that this was the person he wanted to hire, the man with no ears asked, "Do you notice anything unusual about me?" Much to his surprise, the candidate replied, "Yes, you wear contact lenses."

Surprised by his response, the man with no ears said, "That is very perceptive of you How did you know that?"

The candidate replied, "It's hard to wear glasses without any ears."

Panel Interview: All Eyes on You

If you are filled with angst about a one-on-one interview, how would you feel about ten eyeballs staring at you when you walk into a conference room and are led to the hot seat where you will be grilled for at least an hour or two? If you are interviewing for a high-level, six-figure executive position, you will be expected to participate in a panel interview. This type of interview is challenging because the job candidate's skills and competencies are judged and evaluated by many people at one time.

Some companies conduct panel interviews to save time or to get the collective opinion of a panel regarding the candidate. Each member of the panel may be responsible for asking you questions that represent relevancy from their position. They will examine many of the interpersonal skills that were discussed in Chapter 5, including:

Listening skills. The ability to listen actively, which can improve personal relationships by reducing conflicts, strengthening cooperation, and fostering understanding.

Communication skills. The ability to effectively deliver a clear message in a respectful way that has been received and properly understood.

Assertiveness. The ability to directly express your ideas and opinions while considering the needs of others.

Decision making. The ability to determine the proper course of action after evaluating the risks.

Stress management. The ability to manage and respond to stress to prevent or minimize negative physical, mental, and emotional symptoms.

Verbal communication. The ability to use words, either spoken or written, to convey a message.

Non-verbal communication. The ability to send and receive wordless messages via body language, posture, facial expressions, eye contact, and gestures.

Make One-on-One Connections

The key to success is establishing a connection with all of the personalities at the panel interview. Remember that the panel will be composed of people who have different personalities, different attitudes, and different body language. You will need to play up to each person on the panel and form one-on-one connections while appearing confident, grounded, and unflappable during the great inquisition. Do not ignore the quiet person on the panel; this person could have the highest degree of influence on the other interviewers.

The Doctor Is In . . .

"When you are escorted into the conference room where the panel interviewers are already seated and waiting for you, don't grin and

> ask if there is only one emergency exit. 'Boy, I bet this floor would
> be in trouble if someone barricaded that.' Make strong eye contact
> with each one and smile in acknowledgment."

A panel interview is a nerve-wracking experience even for a seasoned
pro to be interrogated by a group of strangers who hold the key to your
future success. Take Tony Young, for example, who asked that his real
name not be used. He received a call on a Saturday morning at 10 a.m.
to come in for a panel interview the following Monday afternoon at an
Internet marketing company in Chicago. "I was excited about the final
interview and realized the company must be serious to call me on a
weekend. But I was very surprised that a panel would interview me. I had
so little time to prepare for it."

That Monday, Tony was greeted by the vice president of human
resources, the company president, the vice president of sales and marketing,
and two high-level marketing gurus. Fortunately, Tony had used the rest
of the weekend to formulate his own crazy good game plan for success in
this final interview stage.

Tony's Crazy Good 10-Point Game Plan

1. When Tony received the phone call on Saturday morning about the
   panel interview on Monday morning, he had the presence of mind to
   ask for the names and job titles of the panel interviewers.
2. Tony researched the panelists on LinkedIn and Facebook, and did an
   Internet search on Google. He boned up on their professional backgrounds and uncovered some common interests and acquaintances.
3. Tony rehearsed responses to potential questions about his interest in
   working at the Internet marketing company, such as the diversity of
   its products, reputation in the community, and how it responded to a
   recent economic crisis.
4. Tony prepared stories to illustrate how he thinks and reacts in
   certain situations. His anecdotes followed a situation–task–action–
   response/achievement format that the panel interviews could understand, easily identify with, and ultimately envision Tony as a key
   player in the organization.

5. Tony prepared some questions to ask each panelist to show thought and interest in the organization. "I'm a thinker, not just a doer. I have a vision I want to share for the company's business future." His curiosity about the company's plans for growth implied a long-term commitment to the company and its future success.

6. Tony's wife, Erica, volunteered her time to rehearse a rigorous battery of practice questions about his past job experiences, career objectives, and a series of hypothetical situations.

7. Erica helped Tony select appropriate interview attire in advance: a stylishly-cut charcoal gray suit, white shirt, red power tie, sleek black leather belt, and black leather slip-ons. The look was polished, but youthful enough to appeal to everyone on the interview panel at the Internet marketing company. Erica went the extra mile by giving Tony a manicure and helping him trim the hair overflowing his ears.

8. Tony printed out extra copies of his resume and slipped them inside his briefcase.

9. Even though Tony has a GPS in his car, he also printed out a map with directions to the interview location.

10. Tony realized that it's important to be calm, cool, and collected during an interview, so he planned to get ample sleep the night before, and give himself plenty of time to drive to the interview.

Real-life result: Tony aced the interview and received a thumbs-up from every member on the interview panel. He accepted the job offer at the Internet marketing company and has been doing great work.

The Doctor Is In . . .

"In a panel interview, always begin your response by making eye contact with the person who asked you the questions. Then make random and soft eye contact with each of the other interviewers. As you finish up your response, return your eye contact to the person who asked you the question. Do not mow down the interviewers by going down the line making eye contact one after the other. Soft random eye contact does the trick."

Turning "You're Fired!" into "You're Hired!"

In some group interviews, a job candidate may be asked to demonstrate her problem-solving skills or make a presentation. The interviewers want to see how the candidate applies her skills and knowledge to a real-life situation, as illustrated in this real-life interview story.

Lee Vikre, former Vice President of Talent and Culture for McMurry, a branded content marketing communications agency in Phoenix, shared her experience in interviewing Heidi Bressler, a past finalist on *The Apprentice*, a popular reality TV show with money mogul Donald Trump.

McMurry holds a minimum of five one-on-one interviews with job candidates, and one final panel interview with a room of five high-powered executives. All of the interviewers were clued in on Bressler's *Apprentice* experience. Even though Trump dismissed finalist Bressler with "You're fired!" she applied her crazy good personality brand to land an advertising sales position with McMurry, culminating the interview process with "You're hired!"

Vikre knew immediately that Heidi Bressler would be either a smashing success or a train wreck in a high-powered advertising sales position for a luxury publication. "She definitely was not a 'C' player," Vikre recalls. She sailed through five one-on-one interviews and received a unanimous thumbs up. The final panel interview included Vikre, the CEO, President, Publisher of *The Ritz-Carlton Magazine*, and the Vice President of Client Services.

Bressler's experience on reality TV served her well—she looked like a young professional who exuded confidence and glamour. Aside from her polished appearance, Bressler was absolutely one of the most flat-out aggressive people that Vikre ever interviewed. She controlled the room in a skillful way and would not take "no" for an answer. She was endearing and exhibited no ego. In fact, after responding to some questions, she would laugh and say, "Silly Heidi. I'm just a little crazy by nature. I have to be authentic . . . I can't be fake." This comment, in particular, caught Vikre's attention, for she can spot someone who lacks authenticity a mile away.

The interviewers tried to rattle Bressler's cage by assimilating real-life experiences that she would face out in the field when trying to close ad sales with clients, but they couldn't shake her. One interviewer perused Bressler's resume and observed that she seemed to be a job-hopper, to which Bressler objected, "Really? Don't call me that. One of the magazines folded." She responded to another question with a lighthearted "You gotta be kidding."

Her attitude was "If Donald Trump couldn't shake me, you can't either. Before I went on the show, I was thick skinned. After the show, I have skin of steel."

At the panel interview, Bressler was required to do a sales presentation for everyone who expected her to try to sell them advertising. Silly interviewers. Bressler pulled out a wild card—an element of surprise—by selling something else. "If I can present and sell myself in front of Donald Trump, I can present to McMurry Inc." She was determined to knock them off their seats and take control of the interview. "If she had any more swagger and ego, it would have been off-putting," says Vikre.

Bressler was hired to sell advertising in *The Ritz-Carlton Magazine*. She works and resides in New York but reports to McMurry's Phoenix office. Recently, she tried to close a sale with one of her New York clients before the ad deadline. He finally agreed, threw his hands up in the air and said, "If you weren't so charming, I'd take out a restraining order."

Crazy Good Panel Interview Tips

- Smile and shake hands firmly with each member of the panel and be sure to repeat their names.
- Spread your attention and make eye contact with each member of the panel as you reply to a question, regardless of who posed it.
- Take your time to compose your response to each question. If a question is unclear, ask for clarification.
- Be aware of panel interactions and nonverbal communication. The leader is the one who other members look at after each of your responses.
- Provide examples of work and volunteer experience that relate to the specific job requirements. Use statistics that demonstrate cost savings, increased productivity and revenue, and reductions in employee absenteeism.
- At the end of the interview, ask the panel when a hiring decision will be made. This question communicates that you may have other job opportunities in the offing.
- Follow up the panel interview with thank-you emails or cards to each interviewer. Collect business cards at the end of the interview, or follow-up with the receptionist regarding email addresses and the correct spelling of each interviewer's name.

Group Interview: When You're One Among Many

Occasionally, an employer will conduct a group interview to uncover the leadership potential of prospective managers and employees who will be dealing with the public; for example, retail store manager trainees. This type of interview usually takes place in an informal setting where the job seekers can learn about the company while interacting with each other.

There is an ulterior motive behind a group interview: The employer is trying to determine which candidates emerge as leaders and which candidates are good followers who can take direction well. In some cases, it's better to be a leader. In other cases, it's better to be task-oriented. It all depends on the type of personality needed to fill the position.

The job candidates will be interviewed as a group, and then individually. In the group stage, there will be a discussion on a work-related situation and a dilemma is raised. The candidates must work together to find a solution.

Your goal is to stand out among the other job seekers, under the watchful eyes of the evaluators. You don't want to come across as too aggressive and off-putting, but you should be friendly and assertive with your team members.

Here are 10 ways to interact successfully with your team members and make a great impression in a group interview:

1. Introduce yourself to the other candidates, and highlight your unique accomplishments.
2. Look interested when others talk.
3. Find a middle road between dominating and cooperating with others.
4. It's appropriate to be a contrarian in order to present a unique perspective.
5. Persuade others to accept your opinion if it's not a popular stance.
6. Support good ideas contributed by your team members.
7. Listen carefully to ideas of your team members.
8. If there is a disagreement, take the role of mediator.
9. Think out of the box to illustrate your creativity.
10. Volunteer to be the team's presenter to the interviewing panel.

10

Head Games

Job candidates often fall victim to head games, the kind an interviewer plays on interviewees, and the kind that interviewees play on themselves. You could be the unwilling recipient of head games during any type of interview discussed in Chapter 9: phone, Skype, one-on-one, panel, and group interviews.

If you have the sneaking suspicion the interviewer is jerking your chain, you are probably right. Unfortunately, some interviewers will play mind games with job candidates to test their reactions. If you are unflappable, you will pass the acid test and may receive a job offer or, at least, be a finalist. If you crumble, then the interviewer will assume you probably cannot handle the stresses of the job. When you can't take the heat, stay out of the kitchen as the saying goes.

Although mind games cannot determine how you would handle stress in a real-life work situation, some interviewers persist in playing them. How can you tell if the interviewer is playing games? Chances are good if he starts challenging your response with pointed statements, such as "You gotta be kidding me." "You really believe that?" "That wouldn't work here at all."

Sometimes interviewers pretend they are mini–psychologists and try to crack open your brain and look inside. They will ask a barrage of questions that begin with "why" or "what." For example: Why would you ever want to work here? What compelled you to accept some of your past jobs? What drives you to do the things you do? What is your underlying motivation?

You will feel like you are being psychoanalyzed, and you are almost tempted to ask, "Do you want me to lie down on the couch for this?"

Games Interviewers Play

You could encounter three types of head games in an interview: The Challenge, The Amateur Psychologist, and The Deadly Choice.

The Challenge: The interviewer responds to your answer with, "There is no way we would do that here." Then, the interviewer will challenge you to see if you will change your mind about your statement, opinion, or belief.

In this game, the interviewer will challenge almost everything you say. The crazy good behavior is to hold your ground and not bend to satisfy the interviewer. In many cases, he or she is looking for someone who is assertive and stands up for himself. In other cases, the interviewer is just plain crazy, and there is nothing you can do about that. Two, however, can play that game. You can jam up the interviewer by saying, "Are all of the employees here like you? How do you characterize your behavior?" You won't get the job, but you will get some satisfaction in knowing that you refused to play the interviewer's stupid game.

The Amateur Psychologist: You will know you have encountered a budding Sigmund Freud if the interviewer says, "It sounds like you have an unresolved anger issue. Do you think you have a problem?"

The interviewer has put you on the defensive, which is not a good interview position. Your crazy good reaction is to turn the tables in this game and put a positive spin on your response. You can do this by saying things like: "What motivates me is to be able to use my talents to the best my ability and in the service of others. How would that philosophy apply to your organization?"

The main thing to remember with Sigmund-types is that sometimes a cigar is a cigar. Take what the interviewer offers and then answer the question in a way that reflects positively on you. Talk about what you want, what motivates or drives you, and the key abilities you have developed and will bring to the position.

The Deadly Choice: The interviewer will ask a question that has only two alternatives, and they are polar opposite. For example, "If you witnessed a staff member doing something that was against company policy, would you fire the employee on the spot or call security to escort the employee from the premises?"

If you do not agree with either option, the crazy good response is not to select one. The interviewer cannot play this game if you refuse to play. If possible, figure out what the interviewer is really asking, and then answer *that* question. For example, if the interviewer is hammering away at you and creating a stressful situation, you can respond with, "In similar situations where the stress level is raised, here is how I conduct my business."

When mind games are being played, do not let interviewers rattle your cage. Describe how you handled stressful situations in the past. If necessary, take a deep, calming breath to reflect on your answer before you respond. When interviewers see that you are impervious to their head games, they will give up and proceed with the interview more normally.

On occasion, the interviewer is not playing head games, but displays some unusual behavior that is jolting. You are not quite sure how to react. The best reaction is no reaction, as illustrated in the following real-life interview.

Rate the Behavior

Using the Psychotron, how would you rate the job candidate's behavior in the following real-life interview?

Pick Me!

An owner of a direct mail marketing agency interviewed a young woman for a copywriter position. She was excited about the prospect of working at the up-and-coming agency, which aligned with her career plan, and she knew many candidates would be vying for the coveted spot. She prepared well for the interview, wore her best interview suit, and assembled a portfolio of her most impressive samples.

When she arrived for her 11 a.m. appointment, the owner informed her it would be a lunch interview. She was a bit surprised, but agreed to accompany him to a swanky restaurant where they were seated at a table with white linens, china, and crystal goblets. As they talked, he started playing with his nose. His finger wandered up his nostril and he began furiously digging for gold (or green)...all the while maintaining eye contact and holding a lively conversation. Then, he wiped his findings on the tablecloth next to his salad fork without batting an eye.

Amazingly, the woman kept her cool and ignored his bad manners although she couldn't believe what she was seeing. Later that day, she received the job offer. She didn't eat much of her spinach salad, though.

The Doctor Is In . . .

"You can only control your own behavior and reactions to an interviewer's off-the-wall behavior. Practice your stoic face and mind your manners. Turning the other cheek is the best thing you can do. It will make for a crazy good story later."

Tension Relievers

If you feel some tension building between you and the interviewer, how should you handle it? Tension can actually be a crazy good thing if you can show how you would resolve that tension. You demonstrate that by incorporating what the interviewer is saying and then weaving that into your response.

You can always say, "It is interesting that you say that. How did you come to think that way?" Then, you will link your answer to the interviewer's response.

Another crazy good technique is to acknowledge what is going on in the interview. You could say something like, "I feel like we got off track somewhere along the way. I would like to move us back to where I mentioned . . . ."

Tension is not, in and of itself, a bad thing. Tension allows for opinions to be stated and discussed. Often it is not so much the position or philosophy of what you say; it is how you came to believe it. So talk about the process of how you came to believe something (e.g., your philosophy of work, how you treat others, how you use your abilities). Use tension to put energy into your interactions with the interviewer. This energy can move the interview process along and keep interest levels high.

How to Keep from Wigging Out

Some people are nervous by nature. They succumb to their own head games by getting worked up before the interview, worrying that they will forget their responses and make a poor impression. If you are a nervous wreck and are going to lose it, how do you regain your composure? Here are some helpful tips:

1. Know where you're going. Get directions to the interview site. If driving, fill up your tank with gas the night before and use your GPS or print out a map. Allow yourself plenty of time to get to the interview. If you are late, it will compound your nervousness.
2. Get out of your head. Most of your constant self-talk messages will be negative, so banish them from your gray matter. Think positively. Talk yourself up. Tell yourself that you are the best candidate for the job and no one will interview as well as you. Focus on your three strengths using the "power of three" that you learned in Chapter 5.
3. Use mental imagery to visualize a top-notch performance. Research shows this method works for athletes.

4. Breathe in deeply through your nose. Oxygen is your best friend. Feel the breath slowly move down to your abdomen, and then exhale. Most people forget to breathe or they breathe shallowly or even hold their breath in short bursts.

5. Do not let the interviewer rush you. You can always say, "Let me reflect for a moment. That questions hits home for me." Then take some time to think about what you want to share. When in doubt, reiterate your top three strengths or your unique value proposition (UVP).

Your main job in the interview is to tell your story and explain your motivation for applying for this particular position. Share three key traits that you developed over time and what you can offer the organization. By focusing on this crazy good interview strategy, you will greatly increase your chances of a successful interview and forget all about being nervous.

The Doctor Is In . . .

"Leave the head games to the experts. Do not allow the interviewer to mess with your head or sidetrack you. Focus on the value you bring to the position and reiterate your unique value proposition (UVP)."

11 | Looking Good . . . Crazy Good

Mark Twain wrote: "Clothes make the man. Naked people have little or no influence on society." Well, nudity has no place in your job search either unless you are auditioning to be an exotic dancer, a nude model, or an adult-film star. Bottom line: Clothing matters.

It's impossible to deny that clothing has a major impact on society. The U.S. clothing stores industry is composed of about 100,000 stores with combined annual revenue of approximately $150 billion in 2010, according to Reuters. Fashion is part of everyday life, and it is always staring you in the face, as evidenced by the numerous fashion magazines that line newsstand shelves and the popularity of fashion-themed reality TV shows like *What Not to Wear*, *Extreme Makeover*, and *Project Runway*.

Our preoccupation with fashion is evident in the English language, too, which is replete with idioms related to clothing, such as:

- Dressed to the nines (dressed flamboyantly with no detail overlooked).
- Dressed to kill (dressed in stylish clothes).
- All dressed up with nowhere to go (something that did not materialize or was postponed).

143

- Dress the part (look suitable for a particular situation or role).
- Dress down (to scold).
- Take your hat off to (respect, admire).
- Keep your shirt on (be patient).
- By the seat of your pants (by sheer luck).
- Get caught with your pants down (unprepared).
- Fill someone's shoes (to assume someone's position).

Exhibiting good fashion sense is absolutely critical for job seekers who are looking for a leg up on the competition during the interview process. Whether you are a young professional embarking on your career of choice, a seasoned professional in career transition, or you are trying to re-enter the workplace after rearing kids, you will be judged immediately by your appearance before you even open your mouth. After all, it's the first thing that human resources directors or hiring managers will notice about you. You will recall that Chapter 3, "First Impressions Are Lasting Impressions," discussed the accuracy of first impressions and the importance of your outward appearance, citing research by Robert Cialdini, Ph.D., of the University of Arizona: "Looking good equals good."

You are a book that will be judged by your cover, and your attire can make or break you. Make your cover as pleasing as possible, so potential employers will want to find out what's inside.

Perceiving Is Believing

What you wear communicates who you are, what you value, and how you feel. Your attire reflects how you want people to perceive you, and how you perceive yourself. Do you take your professional ambitions seriously, or do you have any at all? Does your clothing exude confidence and authority or sexuality and trendiness? Can potential employers imagine you in the job, or do they want to show you to the nearest exit? Do you look like a good fit for the organization's culture? If they like what they see, you have a better chance of getting the job. Even if you say all the right things, you won't get a job offer if you do not have a pleasing appearance.

When two candidates with similar qualifications are running neck and neck for a job opening, clothing is the deciding factor, according to 65 percent of respondents in a survey of 2,000 employers conducted by TK Maxx in 2010, which was cited in Britain's *Daily Mail*. Additionally, 81 percent of respondents indicated that a business suit suggests an organized and efficient individual.

To illustrate, a well-groomed man wearing a tailored suit is more likely to be viewed as a capable professional than a scruffy guy in a stained shirt and wrinkled slacks. Likewise, a woman in a conservative dress and matching blazer will be perceived as a more serious job candidate than someone who shows up wearing a cropped T-shirt and a casual skirt. These perceptions underscore society's fashion obsession.

Appearance is extremely important in business environments where there is customer contact. In other work environments where there is little or no client or customer interaction, it isn't as important. However, you should always put your best foot or shoe forward in a job interview, regardless of the position. Even if you are aware of the organization's casual dress code, you should dress up for the interview unless the employer specifically instructs you otherwise. In fact, most interviewers expect you to dress more formally than usual.

The Doctor Is In . . .

"If you're unsure what type of outfit to wear, it is best to err on the side of caution and be overdressed rather than underdressed. If you start to feel overdressed, it is easier to dress down than dress up."

Don't get your panties in a bunch worrying about what to wear. Just pick up the phone and call the human resources department or the interview scheduler to inquire about recommended attire for job interviews at that company.

Remember, you are marketing yourself as a product and you want your clothing to support your image. Your goal is to get the job, using every tool in your arsenal. So, plan your interview outfit thoughtfully and dress to impress. Once the evaluator has subconsciously deemed your appearance as acceptable and given you a mental thumbs up, the interview will move forward, and you can focus on selling your unique value proposition (UVP).

Putting It All Together

When you dress well, you feel more comfortable and confident physically and psychologically. In addition, you show respect for the interviewer and the interview process itself. As you prepare for your interview, keep these helpful wardrobe tips in mind for men and women.

For Men Only

Unlike women's fashions, men's clothing is more traditional and less affected by fashion trends. In fact, the men's suit has been virtually unchanged in 70 years. Men's necktie widths vary slightly from time to time, but waiting for any noticeable change is like watching grass grow.

Suit Up

One good-quality suit is sufficient for job interviews if that's all you can afford. A two- or three-buttoned, two-piece matched suit in navy blue or charcoal gray is the best and safest choice; black is a little too formal. Subtle pinstripes are permissible as they can jazz up a gray suit. You will look amateurish if you try to combine a suit jacket with pants that don't match. Four-button suits seem too trendy, and three-piece suits are just plain ostentatious. Could you try any harder?

Suits typically have tacking stitches to hold the back jacket vents in place before the garment is purchased. Be sure to cut them off before your interview. Also, the tag stitched on the outer sleeve is not a Tommy Hilfiger label that is part of the overall design You'd better cut it off or risk embarrassment, as the fellow did in the scenario below.

Rate the Behavior

Using the Psychotron, how would you the rate the job candidate's behavior in the following real-life interview?

Dressed to the Nines

A man in his early 30s interviewed for a ramp position at a major airlines. He arrived projecting a professional appearance. He was well-groomed, clean cut, and wore a very expensive-looking suit, shirt, tie, and polished dress shoes. He was clearly nervous and trying to do his best to charm the interviewer and say all the right things. During the interview, the human resources director noticed that the label was still sewn on the sleeve of the man's new jacket.

Was this crazy bad behavior because the applicant did not attend to details, or is it crazy good behavior because he purchased a suit in order to make a good impression at the interview?

Real-life result: He got the job.

Keep Your Shirt On

A crisp, white long-sleeved shirt is your safest option, even in summer. You can also wear a long-sleeved shirt in a solid light blue, cream, or almond. Dark shirts are too trendy for conservative industries, such as banking and accounting, and are reminiscent of the tough guys in *The Sopranos, The Godfather*, or *Goodfellas*.

Never wear a short-sleeved shirt with a tie unless you're striving for the *Dilbert* comic-strip character look, or you are aspiring to a career in fast-food service. Do not put any pens in your shirt pocket.

Buckle Up

Your belt should match your shoes in color and texture. Large belt buckles are not professional and will clash with your suit. Stick with a classic look that goes with everything.

Tie Breakers

Wear a pure silk tie with a traditional pattern or opt for a classic red power tie. Save the character ties for holidays and other festive occasions. Your tie should reach your beltline. Do not wear a bow-tie to an interview, or you will look like a rube or Orville Redenbacher.

You're a Shoe In

Invest in a pair of high-quality, black or cordovan leather shoes that lace up or slip on, and be sure to break them in before the interview. Black shoes will match any suit, and are easy to coordinate with a belt. Leave your loafers at home. Your socks should match your trousers and be long enough so that the skin on your shin doesn't show if you cross your legs. A hairy calf is a major turn-off during an interview.

Finishing Touches

Wear a conservative watch and a wedding ring if you're hitched. A college ring is acceptable if you're a recent college grad. Small, conservative cufflinks will jazz up your shirt.

Hair's to You

Your hair should be clean, neat, and tidy. Get a haircut, if necessary. Shorter hair is preferred in conservative industries, such as accounting, banking, law, and medicine. For interviews in these sectors, it's best to save the brightly colored Mohawk for Halloween. Facial hair is discouraged, although well-groomed mustaches are usually acceptable.

Making Scents of It All

Be considerate of your interviewer, particularly if your meeting is going to be held in a small conference room. Use cologne sparingly, or none at all. Your interviewer might be hypersensitive or allergic to fragrances.

Just in Case

A small leather briefcase or portfolio is recommended to carry your resume and any job-related materials. Do not carry a large briefcase.

The Doctor Is In . . .

"Do some dress rehearsals in your interview clothes before the 'big day' to ensure they're comfortable and don't restrain your movements. Practice gesturing and raising your arms above your head. If the fabric pulls or your midriff shows, wear a different jacket or shirt."

For Women Only

Suit Yourself

A formal interview suit is appropriate for a conservative professional job interview. Go for a simple and chic look if you're interviewing in a conservative industry like accounting, finance, law, or consulting, or if you aren't sure about the dress code for your interview. You can't go wrong with a basic black skirt-suit (a skirt and blazer made of the same material), white collared shirt, black pumps, nude pantyhose, and a black handbag. Neutrals, such as black, gray, brown, caramel, beige, olive, and navy are all excellent choices for your suit.

In creative fields, such as advertising, public relations, graphic design, and retail, what to wear for an interview might be less clear, and you have more leeway with colors and accessories while still looking professional. The general rule of thumb is subtle, not wacky or tacky. Of course, there are always exceptions to the rule, as in the cases of Susan Boyle and Landau Eugene Murphy, Jr., who were mentioned in Chapter 3, or as illustrated in the following example.

Rate the Behavior

Using the Psychotron, how would you rate the job candidate's attire in the following real-life interview?

Basic Black

A casting coordinator at a major television studio in Los Angeles was interviewing candidates for an internship. Interns come and go, and they are usually upbeat, talkative, high-energy people pleasers who are impeccably dressed and fit the mold of eager, aspiring entertainment executives. Unfortunately, they never seem to work out well.

Imagine her surprise when an intern applicant walked in decked out completely in black: black plaid dress, black hoodie, and black tights. She had a sleek black updo with bangs that completely covered one eye, a big black bow perched on the side of her head, heavy makeup, tattoos, and piercings. Despite her somewhat shocking appearance, she acted very relaxed and low key. The casting coordinator observed that the candidate seemed genuine and comfortable in her own skin. She took up a lot of space in her chair, a subtle indication of her confidence. To her credit, she had internships at other studios and was very familiar with the job responsibilities.

Real-life result: The woman in black was hired on the spot because the casting coordinator had a gut feeling about her. She wanted someone who was "chill" and would keep her head down and do the work.

The black outfit pushed the envelope; other job interviews in non-corporate environments require a dressy version of business casual attire; for example, a simple, sleeveless dress under a jacket. Just adding a jacket to your dress or blouse and skirt can kick up your look a notch.

Word to the wise job hunter: Don't confuse club attire with business attire. If you would wear it to a lounge or a cocktail party, it is not appropriate for a business environment.

Skirt the Issue

If you choose to wear a skirt with a matching jacket or blazer, a slim skirt will project a polished and professional look. Leave your A-line, flared, and wrap skirts in the closet. They have no business in a job interview. Try on the skirt at home and practice walking around and sitting in it. When you sit down, it should still cover your thighs. If this isn't the case, comb your closet for a longer skirt.

If the Shoe Fits

Women should wear high-quality, closed-toed shoes in black, navy, gray, or neutral shades. You can wear black shoes with navy blue or gray suits. Classic pumps or sling-backs are excellent choices, but not the extremely high-heeled shoes that are all the rage and best suited for a nightclub or a costume party. Boots are another no-no for job interviews. If you want to wear new shoes, make sure to break them in before the interview.

Ban the Bling

Your goal is to shoot for understated elegance. Limit your accessories and avoid anything that is too flashy, gaudy, noisy, or oversized. It's simply too distracting for the interviewer. A watch, wedding ring, eyeglasses, and small earrings are foolproof whereas chunky necklaces, glitzy headbands, bulky bracelets, and billowy scarves will just get in the way.

Give Yourself a Hand

Your hands are visible in an interview, so make them extra nice and appealing. Short nails with neutral nail polish (or no nail polish) are best. Moisturize them before the interview, so you're ready to shake hands confidently with your interviewer.

Baggin' It

Carry a simple, classic handbag in a neutral shade or a deep red to punch up your interview attire. You also should invest in a classy tote bag to accommodate all of your job-related materials and personal essentials.

Face It: Make (Up) My Day

Circus clowns can get away with heavy makeup, but women preparing for a job interview should keep theirs to a minimum. The phrase "less is more" applies here. You should strive for a polished and professional appearance, while still looking fresh and natural.

1. Your eyebrows frame your eyes, so banish the uni-brow. Tweeze those unwanted, stray eyebrow hairs for a tidier look.
2. Cover dark eye circles and blemishes with a concealer.
3. Use foundation to even out blotchy skin.
4. Apply a little blush for a healthy, natural glow.
5. Dust with translucent powder to reduce shine.
6. Apply a neutral eye shadow in cream, beige or taupe. Do not try to achieve a smoky, cabaret-singer look.
7. Wear mascara and a thin line of smudged eyeliner pencil. Skip the liquid eyeliner because it's too harsh for an interview.
8. Wear a neutral, matte-finish lipstick rather than shiny lip gloss. Do not outline your lips with a dark lip pencil unless you want to look like a cheap ho. Check for lipstick on your teeth just before you go into your interview. (It's almost as bad as broccoli.)

9. Examine your makeup in broad daylight to get the real picture. Otherwise, you might horrify your interviewer with your garish, mask-like appearance.
10. Keep your nails short and manicured for the job interview.

Hairdo's and Don'ts

If you're not sure how to wear your hair for a job interview, turn on the TV and check out the local newscasters. If your hair is short, you simply can't go wrong with a classic style, such as a bob (one length, layered, or inverted). If you have long hair, experiment with a braid, twist, bun, or a sleek ponytail, but avoid distracting hair ornaments.

Your hair color should be subdued to avoid being stereotyped as a dumb blonde or a wild and crazy redhead. Play it safe with sandy blonde, soft brown, or brunette shades.

Strive for a smooth, sophisticated look that doesn't require a lot of upkeep. Avoid teasing your hair out to there, or the interviewer might wonder if you have just stuck a fork into an electrical outlet. Enough said.

Tits, Tats, and Body Piercings

If you're a female who is taking inventory of her clothes closet to select the right interview outfit for the big day, you would be wise to avoid the booby trap. You can flaunt your cleavage when you're painting the town red on a Friday or Saturday night or if you are interviewing at Hooters, but it is totally inappropriate for a corporate job interview. In fact, showing up with even a hint of cleavage could cost you the job, according to the 2010 survey of 2,000 employers conducted by TK Maxx, which was cited in Britain's *Daily Mail.*

Your intellect, education, job experience, and skills should take center stage at a job interview, not your Juggernauts. Keep your blouse buttoned up so the interviewer can focus on what you're saying, not on what you're displaying. Otherwise, your interviewer may be so distracted by your breasts that you might end up saying, "Hey, I'm up here!"

Rate the Behavior

Using the Psychotron, how would you rate the job hunter's selection of interview attire in the following real-life anecdote?

Enough Sleaze to Please

A woman in her late 20s was getting dressed to interview for the position of administrative assistant to the president of a large corporation—a 40-something male. Her qualifications weren't up to snuff, but somehow she landed the interview. Before she left her apartment to drive to the interview, she asked her roommate, a human resources manager at a small company, how she looked. Her roommate tried to hide her shock when she saw the woman's see-through white blouse with black bra underneath, tight skirt, and five-inch heels. "Well, that outfit would be great if you were going to a nightclub, but it's not appropriate interview attire."

The job seeker snapped back, "*This* is how I'm going to get the job."

The next day, the woman received the job offer despite her lack of top-notch skills. In this particular case, the little brain hired her. Rumor has it that she had an affair with her boss and broke up his marriage. And she never did receive the promotions and other perks that he continually dangled in front of her nose.

Word of caution: Your attire reflects your professionalism. Do not put yourself in a compromising position by conveying the wrong message about yourself and your work ethic. Eventually, it will bite you in the behind.

Tattoos

Today, many professional athletes, rock stars, entertainers, movie stars, models, and other high-profile figures sport tattoos. The Food and Drug Administration (FDA) estimates that 45 million Americans have at least one tattoo. The popularity of body art has increased dramatically since 1976 when only 1 percent of all Americans had a least one tattoo, compared to 25 percent of the U.S. population in 2006, according to the Society for Human Resource Management (SHRM).

Despite the increasing popularity of tattoos, they will thwart your climb up the career ladder, especially in conservative industries, such as banking, law, medicine, accounting, and insurance. Dress codes have loosened in some industries, and employers in marketing, advertising, sales, graphic design, and technology, are more likely to accept fashion trends, like tattoos and even body piercings, in the workplace. The bottom line, however, is that you don't look like you mean business when there's a snake, a skull, or barbed wire emblazed on your forearm or neck. Even if you're wearing a crisp, white long-sleeved shirt, you cannot conceal tattoos on your face, neck, and hands.

People aged 18 to 29 consider tattoos—and body piercings, including tongue rings—as fashion accessories while older individuals view them as badges of badness rather than decorative designs. The statistics below, from a 2006 Pew Research Center study, find more than one-third of people aged 18 to 45 have tattoos, while the percentage of those with body piercings is also rising in the younger generations.

Generation	Percent with Tattoos	Percent with Body Piercings
Millennials, 18–29	38	23
Generation X, 30–45	32	9
Baby Boomers, 46–64	15	1
Silents (65+)	6	N/A

Source: Pew Research Center.

Nearly 40 percent of adults aged 18 to 40 now have a tattoo or non-earlobe piercing, according to the Pew Research Center's GenNext Survey. And those visible displays of personal style sometimes clash with company-appearance policies and perceptions of what older bosses expect of younger workers.

Tattoos still carry a stigma as many people associate them with a rougher, less educated class of people, such as bikers, sailors, criminals, ex-convicts, gang members, and the dregs of society. In fact, 85 percent of survey respondents believe that tattoos and body piercings impede a job seeker's chances of getting hired, according to career publisher Vault.com's Employee Tattoo and Body Piercing Survey, conducted in July 2007. Sixty percent of employers said that they were less likely to hire a candidate with tats or piercings. The survey also revealed that 70 percent of the people with tattoos whom they surveyed concealed them at work. The survey drew responses from 468 employees in a variety of industries across the States. For more information, visit www.vault.com.

Tattoos might be symbols of self-expression to you, but some potential employers will immediately assume that you are rebellious and not a team player. Employers feel that employees with tattoos might tarnish the company's squeaky-clean reputation, offend clients, startle customers, and frighten small children. This is especially true for jobs that involve client interaction or customer service, like retail stores and restaurants.

Body art, like tattoos, is distracting to interviewers. It's best to keep your tattoos covered when you're trying to get hired. You can hide them by wearing long sleeves or using a cosmetic concealer that's made specifically for this purpose, like Dermablend®. Find a shade to match your skin tone, dab it on, and watch the tattoo magically disappear until you scrub it off with soap and water. You should also check out a concealer kit offered on www.Tattoocamo.com.

The Doctor Is In . . .

"Job candidates without tattoos and piercings are more marketable. Cover visible tats and remove visible piercings to make a more favorable impression in the interview."

Tattoos are not an employment issue unless they are visible. Many workers realize this, so those with body art on their torsos, arms, ankles or necks cover their exposed tattoos with long pants, long-sleeved shirts and other work-appropriate clothing.

Your company can't use tats or piercings as an excuse to fire you. On the flipside, a company can use them as excuses not to hire you. Employers are allowed to impose dress codes and appearance policies as long as they do not discriminate on race, color, religion, age, national origin, or gender, according to the Equal Employemnt Opportunity Commission. Tattoos and body piercings do not fall under EEOC's protective umbrella.

Many companies have policies that prohibit tats and piercings that are outlined in their handbook and/or employee manual. An employer may change a dress code at any time, with or without warning. To cover their butts legally, employees usually will distribute the new guidelines in written form. If an employer does change the dress code, it must be applicable to all employees.

While society and popular culture are changing, workplace rules and regulations still lag behind what is considered hip and in. Many companies prohibit visible tattoos, but the increasing number of Generation X and Y workers sporting them could lead to a change in businesses' attitudes toward body art. Before indulging in ink and metal, job seekers should contact potential employees to inquire if tattoos and piercings are acceptable in the work environment.

The following companies allow visible tattoos that are not offensive, according to www.tat2x.com, a site that continually provides updates on employers that permit or prohibit visible tattoos and body piercing.

Barnes & Noble
Bath & Body Works
Ford Motor Company
Kohl's Department Stores
Nationwide Insurance
Target
Teavana
Wahoo's
Walmart

The employers listed below prohibit visible tattoos. Go to www.tat2x.com for regular updates on the site's blog.

Abercrombie & Fitch
Albertson's Grocery Store

AMC Theaters
Banfield Pet Hospital (associated with Petsmart)
Blockbuster Video
The Body Shop
Burger King
Calvin Klein
CEC Entertainment | Chuck E. Cheese's
The Cheesecake Factory
Coco's Bakery Restaurant
The Coffee Bean and Tea Leaf
Comcast Cable
Costco
Crabtree & Evelyn
Dairy Queen
Denny's Restaurant
DIRECTV
Disney Store
Enterprise Rent-A-Car
Express Fashions
Friendly's
Geico Insurance
KFC
Little Caeser's Pizza
McDonald's
Movie Gallery
Office Depot
Olive Garden
Oregano's Pizza Bistro
Panera Bread
PetSmart
Pier 1 Imports
Pizza Hut
Princess Cruises
Queen Mary 2
RadioShack
Red Robin Restaurant
Regal Entertainment Group
Ritz Carlton Hotels
Safeway

Starbucks
Six Flags Amusement Parks
Starwood Hotels
Suncoast Motion Pictures
Sunglass Hut
Swiss Chalet
Toys "R" Us
UltraStar Cinemas
Unites States Postal Service
Van Heusen
VCA Animal Hospitals
VNA of Care New England
Victoria's Secret
Zaxbys

The Doctor Is In . . .

"Three things you don't want to hear a tattoo artist say:
  'Dog? I thought you said hog.'
  'I hate having the hiccups when I'm working.'
  'Oops! I hope this needle is clean.'"

12 | Use Body Language to Make a Crazy Good Impression

You have heard the expression, "It's not what you say—it's how you say it." Well, that is not entirely accurate. Your nonverbal cues are just as important as your verbal ones. In fact, your likeability factor is based on approximately 10 percent of your verbal communication. Your tone of voice accounts for 30 percent, and the remaining 60 percent of your likeability is derived from your nonverbal communication—your body language—which includes eye contact, posture, gestures, and facial expressions.

You can learn how to use your body language to enhance your verbal communication and send a positive message to your interviewer, but in order to change your body language, you must be aware of it. Do you make eye contact? Do you stand up straight and sit tall? Do you use your hands and facial expressions to emphasize important points? By using body language to your advantage, you will be remembered as a job candidate who made a great first impression by appearing comfortable and at ease.

Make Crazy Good Eye Contact

Eye contact is very important when you are interviewing for a job. Individuals who maintain eye contact create a favorable impression because they exude confidence and social aptitude. When you look someone straight in the eye while you are conversing, you are perceived as honest and trustworthy. It is also a sign of respect because your interviewer knows he has your undivided attention when your eyes are focused on him.

On the other hand, there is a delicate balance between using too much or too little eye contact. You should maintain firm eye contact when you are introduced to interviewers, shake hands, and answer job-related questions. By smiling and maintaining eye contact when shaking hands, you will appear warm, friendly, approachable, and interested. You can supplement your eye contact with an occasional smile and a nod of the head to look more natural. Caution: if you nod too much or too vigorously, you will look like a bobble-head. Just try to relax and be yourself.

One-on-One Interview

In a one-on-one interview, use an eye clasp to lock eyes with the interviewer for three to five seconds and then release. You should alternate your gaze between the interviewer's eyes, forehead, and the bridge of the nose. But, what if your interviewer is wall-eyed, and has one eye that looks straight ahead and the other eye looks off to the side, upward, or downward? Which eye do you look at? This is an age-old question that has been on everyone's mind at one time or another. Answer: you should focus on the eye that's looking directly at you. By knowing how to handle your interviewer's wayward eye, you will be able to sail through the interview unshaken.

Panel Interview

In a panel interview, you must make eye contact with everyone in the room even if it's only for a few seconds. Otherwise, some of the interviewers will feel ignored or slighted and harbor resentment for you. This will work to your disadvantage when it comes time for the interviewers to make a hiring decision.

If an interviewer asks a difficult question, look him in the eye and regularly move your gaze to other interviewers in the room when you are responding to the question, but do not look rapidly from one person to another like you are watching a Ping-Pong tournament. As you wrap up your answer, return your gaze to the person who asked the question.

It is only natural to glance upward when recalling information that you will use in formulating your response to the interviewer's question. Your face should always match what you're saying or about to say, so be sure that your facial expression is pensive and reflective to indicate that you're giving serious consideration to your response.

The Doctor Is In . . .

"If your eyes dart back and forth, you will appear shifty eyed, sneaky, and untrustworthy. Focus on the interviewer for best results. Make direct and soft eye contact."

Lack of Eye Contact

You should not let your eyes wander around the room when the interviewer is talking even if the collage on the wall is more interesting than his monologue. Put yourself in the interviewer's role. Have you ever talked to someone who was staring off in the distance? How did it make you feel? He certainly wasn't concentrating on what you were saying. Perhaps you even turned around to see what he was looking at. Conversely, if you are the one who is focusing on something besides the interviewer, you will look like you are daydreaming. Certainly, you don't want to give the impression that you're bored to death, or you would spend the workday with your head in the clouds instead of doing your job.

If you look away while answering questions, it is a subtle indication that your words may not be truthful. The interviewer also might assume that you lack confidence and are unqualified to do the job effectively. If you look intimidated or afraid, you will bomb the interview, regardless of your stellar job experience or academic record. The interviewer will fear that you are the type to run away at the first sign of trouble, instead of using proactive problem-solving skills.

Staring You Right in the Face

Avoid staring at the interviewer without blinking, or you will make him feel very uneasy and self-conscious. When you give the big, hairy eyeball, you are encroaching on the interviewer's space. A constant stare indicates mistrust; for example, you just can't take your eyes off the interviewer. Just as in the animal kingdom, a stare down is an act of aggression leading to a direct physical attack. Don't make your interviewer fear that you are invading his territory and you are going to pounce on him at any moment.

If you are concerned about your use of eye contact, videotape a mock interview with a friend and then watch it. Pay attention to your eye contact when you respond to some typical questions. Take note of where you look when you break eye contact and train yourself not to look down. Practice until you are a star pupil on the subject of making good eye contact.

Rate the Behavior

Using the Psychotron, how would you rate the job candidate's behavior in the following real-life interview?

Roving Eyes

A magazine editor at a non-profit association interviewed a recent college grad for the position of editorial assistant. The candidate had a journalism degree and excellent writing samples. While the magazine editor gave a brief overview of the association and the job responsibilities, the candidate's eyes darted around the room impatiently. She would not maintain eye contact even when responding to interview questions. At the end of the interview, she yawned. The next day, the magazine editor received an email from the candidate, thanking her for the interview and conveying her keen interest and enthusiasm for the job.

Did the job candidate exhibit crazy good behavior by displaying interest in the interviewer's office décor, or crazy bad behavior because she appeared totally disengaged in the meeting?

Real-life result: In spite of her top-notch writing samples, the candidate was not hired purely because of her lack of eye contact and her big, fat yawn.

Posture Perfect

"Head up, shoulders back." Remember when your mother, grandmother, teacher, or other well-meaning adult told you to stand straight when you were a kid? You found their nagging irritating at times, but little did you know that good posture can improve your chances of getting a job offer.

Good posture conveys an upbeat attitude and reflects high energy, enthusiasm, and leadership potential. Even if you are short in stature, you can project confidence and authority by standing and sitting tall, with a straight back and squared shoulders. The same applies to tall people. Nothing looks worse than a tall person who is slumped over.

Adopting a confident, expansive stance can be the deciding factor in landing a coveted job, according to studies conducted in 2009 by the Kellogg School of Management at Northwestern University. The research found that when you carry yourself proudly and take up more space, you will feel more confident and powerful, regardless of your rank in an organization.

In one study, undergraduate students who occupied more space when seated (by extending their arms and crossing one leg over the knee), scored higher on power, abstract thinking, and willingness to act. In contrast, undergraduates who sat in restricted positions in which they did not take up much space (dropped shoulders, hands under thighs, and feet together) did not perform as well as their space-craving counterparts.

Good posture also makes you feel better about yourself, according to another study of 71 students conducted in 2009 by Richard Petty, professor of psychology at the Ohio State University, Pablo Briñol, a former postdoctoral fellow at Ohio State, and Benjamin Wagner, a graduate student at Ohio State.

If you were the interviewer, would you hire the job candidate with good posture who appears to be a vibrant picture of health, or a sloucher who looks gloomy and submissive? Interestingly, there is a connection between bad posture and depression. Bad posture can create depression, and depression can lead to a bad posture. Depressed people shuffle slowly with their heads down, eyes downcast, hunched shoulders, and rounded back.

Many people have poor posture due to bad habits, such as hunching over a computer keyboard for umpteen hours a day, year after year. This closed posture makes individuals appear submissive, less confident, and lacking in leadership skills. Don't despair if your current posture is not ram-rod straight. Your bad posture does not destine you to look like Quasimodo in *The Hunchback of Notre-Dame*, the lumbering bell ringer at the Notre-Dame Cathedral in Paris, in Victor Hugo's famous novel.

If you slouch, you can improve your posture by reminding yourself to stand tall with your head up, your chin tucked, your shoulders back, your chest raised, and your pelvis tilted forward, while holding in your stomach. It sounds like a lot to remember, but practice makes habit.

Sitting Pretty

The proper sitting position will make you feel comfortable, balanced, and relaxed, and appear professional, confident, and in control to the interviewer. When you are ushered into the interviewer's office or a conference room and invited to have a seat, you should assume the tell position in the chair, which is composed of the following elements:

- Sit up straight.
- Keep your head and chin up.
- Square up your shoulders.
- Keep your arms at your side or on the chair armrests.
- Center yourself on the chair.
- Distribute your weight evenly.

- Relax your back against the back of the chair
- Plant your feet firmly.
- Spread your feet or cross your ankles.
- Lean forward slightly to show interest.
- Take up as much space as possible in the chair to project an air of confidence.

This tell posture encourages you to look directly into the interviewer's eyes when speaking. Proper posture also aligns your body, so you can speak clearly from your diaphragm and project your words when talking to the interviewer. After you answer each question, return to your original tell sitting position.

You should avoid using negative body language while seated during the interview, including the following:

- Sitting with your arms crossed is a defensive position.
- Imitating *The Thinker* is hokey.
- Sitting too far to the left or right makes you look like the Leaning Tower of Pisa.
- Crossing and uncrossing your legs repeatedly is distracting.
- Bouncing your knees is an irritating, nervous habit.
- Leaning too far forward makes you look anxious and tense, or like you're getting too personal (based on other gestures).
- Sitting too far back in the chair suggests a cavalier attitude, which may be more appropriate near the end of the interview.

Rate the Behavior

Using the Psychotron, how would you rate the job candidate's behavior described in the following real-life interview?

Drawing the Wrong Conclusion

It was right after the various shootings that had occurred on numerous university campuses when a medical school candidate arrived for his set of interviews. The university had recently installed an alert system, and people were in high-awareness mode.

He was dressed in the usual male garb: dark suit, shirt, prep tie, and polished shoes. He also looked a tad more nervous than most of the other interviewees.

As the candidate got settled into the chair and the interviewer was about to ask her first question, the candidate slowly moved his hand towards his inside jacket pocket. The interviewer quickly asked her first question and the candidate moved his hand back to the armrest on his chair and answered the question.

The interviewer was about to ask her next question when she noticed the same movement of his hand. She quickly asked her question and saw his hand withdraw.

This pattern repeated itself for the next three questions with the interviewer getting more and more anxious. She wondered what was in his coat pocket and if she should be worried that he might draw a concealed weapon.

Finally, the interviewer told the candidate that she noticed that each time she was about to ask a question, the candidate started to move his hand toward his inside pocket. She then asked, "Do you have something in your pocket that you want to show me?"

The candidate nodded and reached into his pocket. The interviewer had her hand poised over her alarm button. She sighed with relief when the candidate pulled out some photographs documenting his recent experience working in a health clinic overseas.

Was the candidate's behavior crazy good because he brought photos depicting his time spent overseas, or was it crazy bad behavior for making hand gestures that could be construed as threatening?

Mirror Image

If you feel awkward during the interview, you should mirror the interviewer's posture and body language. Mirroring body language is a powerful tool for building trust, rapport, and understanding by putting the other person at ease almost instantly. This technique is valuable in business, sales, friendships, and in job interviews. You can form immediate connections by mirroring posture, gestures, sitting position, tone of voice, and pace of talking.

When you are being open and honest, you will tend to adopt the same stances as the person whose trust you are trying to gain. Mirroring is natural and instinctive; for example, you yawn when you see someone yawn. You smile when someone smiles at you. A smile is a nonverbal acknowledgment of understanding, and the simplest form of mirroring body language. People feel good when they see people smile, so keep smiling.

Mirroring makes people feel understood and in agreement. When people have rapport, they will match each other's body language and facial expressions. In other words, they will subconsciously mirror each other. They see themselves in their own reflection. Think of people attending a wedding, a graduation, a parade, a rock concert, or a funeral. They are subconsciously connected and share the same body language and emotions. They feel part of the whole group dynamic.

Rate the Behavior

Using the Psychotron, how would you rate the job candidate's behavior described in the following real-life interview?

Let's Be Friends

When the Director of Corporate Communications for a giftware manu-facturing and licensing company interviewed a woman for the position of Director of Public Relations, she took an instant liking to her. The job candidate brought two portfolios of her work and sat right beside her, explaining her impressive samples in detail as she flipped through them page by page. The interviewer was highly impressed, and observed that the job candidate behaved more like a close friend, instead of someone vying for a high-level corporate position.

Was the job candidate's behavior crazy bad for acting chummy and informal, or crazy good because her friendliness and body language helped establish an immediate rapport with the interviewer?

Real-life result: The candidate exhibited similar behavior in her one-on-one interviews with other people at the company, who absolutely loved her warm approach. Everyone agreed unanimously to hire her.

Your mirroring technique must be very subtle and unnoticeable. To use it successfully, you should not copycat the interviewer's gestures or facial expressions immediately, which would be too obvious. Wait 10 or 15 seconds before using similar body language. Copycatting can be very annoying if it is not handled correctly, as this example shows: When you were a kid, you probably teased and mimicked your pals on occasion, to which they responded, "Stop copying me!" This type of mirroring did not build rapport; it started fistfights. Now fast forward to your interview. You wouldn't want to be ordered out of the interviewer's office for copycatting, would you?

Watch your interviewer closely. If he is using hand gestures, you should do the same. Conversely, if your interviewer is not using hand gestures, avoid using them yourself. Speak at the same pace or slower than your interviewer, so you do not appear tense and harried. Mirroring is a two-way street, and your interviewer may feel compelled and pressured to match your fast pace of talking.

Gestures and Facial Expressions

Your energy, excitement, and enthusiasm are the foundation of effective communication. When you combine facial expressions with hand gestures, you can set the tone or mood for the interview, support and emphasize your points, make it easy for the interviewer to follow your verbal responses, and communicate your authenticity. By aligning your hand gestures with your words, you can drive home key points that you want to make.

The Doctor Is In . . .

"Use gestures to paint a picture with your hands and give some visual stimuli. Show action through your gestures."

The right gestures and facial expressions inspire trust and can make a good impression on the interviewer. Gestures, either conscious or subconscious, express your thoughts more clearly than the words that you speak. Understanding gestures can help you deal more effectively with your interviewers and the people in your everyday life.

Give Yourself a Hand

A firm handshake is critical when you are interviewing or networking. It's the first gesture you make in the interview, and it is your last gesture when the interview ends. It should reflect a capable professional, not a timid, mild-mannered individual or an aggressive, heavy-handed blowhard.

A confident handshake consists of three to four short pumps. It should be delivered in a face-to-face standing position, unless the other person is seated, and enhanced by a smile and warm remarks, such as "Hello, Dr. Molidor. I'm Barbara Parus. It's a pleasure meeting you. I look forward to learning more about the ABC Company."

After your interview, you should smile, shake hands again, and close with something like, "Thanks for taking the time to meet with me. I hope I have shown you how I can be a valuable asset to your company."

Will you be remembered as the job candidate with stellar qualifications and an assertive handshake, or will your handshake become an amusing topic of conversation for the human resources department because it falls into one of the following categories?

The Hook: A finger-only, claw-like grasp
The Limp Noodle: A clammy, moist handshake
The Brush-off: A barely-there, palm-brushing motion
The Tight Squeeze: A bone-breaking, knuckle-cracking grip
The Water Pump: A vigorous, up-and-down pumping action

Here are more body language tips for your interview that might convey subconscious messages:

- Showing your palms indicates sincerity.
- Holding your palms downward is a sign of dominance. Do not shake hands with your palms down.
- Pressing the fingertips of your hands together to form a church steeple is a display of confidence.
- Concealing your hands, as in putting them in your pockets, is a sign that you have something to hide.
- Finger tapping is a sign of impatience.
- Folding your arms across the chest is a very defensive position, indicating disappointment or disagreement.
- Overusing hand gestures to the point of distraction.

Head and Shoulders

The way you hold your head reflects your mindset. Keep this body language in mind at your next interview:

- Touching your ear or scratching your chin is sign that you don't buy the bull.
- Tilting your head forward is a sign of shyness.
- Tilting your head backward shows overconfidence or pride.
- Tilting your head slightly to the side shows you are friendly and ready to listen.
- Tilting your head to one side could be construed as boredom.
- Glazed eyes staring straight ahead indicate boredom (or a hangover).
- Excessive blinking is a sign of lying.
- A harsh or blank facial expression indicates hostility.
- Shrugging your shoulders could be viewed as willingness to unload a problem or burden, or a sign of impatience or total detachment.

In your next job interview, pay special attention to your gestures as they could help in increasing your chances of getting the job.

The Doctor Is In . . .

"If you're excited, let your face show it. Look for opportunities to communicate your personality and emphasize points by smiling and using other positive facial expressions."

13 | Voiceovers: Your Voice Speaks Volumes

Do you remember sitting in a classroom fighting to stay awake while your college professors lectured? You even wished you had a couple of toothpicks handy to prop your eyelids open, so you looked like you were awake and paying attention. Often, it wasn't the content that was ridiculously boring, but rather the lackluster delivery of the information. The professors droned, showing their own lack of enthusiasm for their topics. If they sounded bored with their own subject matter, how could you possibly muster up any enthusiasm?

But, what if they had infused energy and excitement into their voices, peppered with variations in pace and volume, some strategically placed pauses, and corresponding facial expressions and hand gestures to add emphasis? Instantly, they would have grabbed their students' attention. By injecting exuberance into their voices, they could transform a boring presentation into ear candy. The audience would hang on every word and want to hear more.

Now, imagine a similar scenario in a hiring manager's office. The first job candidate walks in and slithers quietly into a chair. She speaks in a soft, hushed voice, so low that the interviewer must crane his neck forward to hear her. Her meek demeanor immediately raises doubts and concerns about her ability to do the job effectively. The next job candidate marches in confidently, and clearly states his name and his unique value proposition (UVP). Within seconds, he instills confidence in the interviewer.

Lesson: Your voice is a powerful interviewing tool. Learn to use it to your advantage.

It's not enough to have an impressive resume that highlights academic achievements and previous job experience. Many job applicants mistakenly assume that if they have a glowing resume, and they respond correctly to the interviewer's questions, they will be handed a job offer on a silver platter or, at the very least, they will feel they are in the running for the job. You know what they say about the word "assume": It makes an "ass" out of "u" and "me." True, the content of the responses is extremely important, but the tone of voice is equally important.

Your tone of voice sets the atmosphere during an interview by projecting your inner confidence, your vitality, and your authority. An interviewee can use all of the right words in his or her responses, but if the answers aren't delivered with confidence, the interviewer won't buy them. When you are confident, people can hear it in your voice. You deliver your message loud and clear with conviction.

Your voice conveys your personality, and people form immediate impressions of you based on your voice. A Stanford University study found that people can hear personality in the voices of others, and the sound of one's voice influences opinions about everything from credibility to sexual prowess.

The Doctor Is In . . .

"When your voice radiates confidence, people will feel confident about you."

Your voice and speech are as unique as your fingerprints. You are judged by the sound of your voice and the clarity of your speech in job interviews, business meetings, and at social occasions. Your voice is a persuasive tool that is often neglected when preparing for job interviews. Truth be told, job applicants spend more time choosing their interview attire than they do rehearsing their verbal responses. How about you? How many hours have you dwelled on what shoes (or tie, handbag, or scarf) to wear with your interview suit, compared to the time you have invested in practicing your responses aloud to potential interview questions? Your voice communicates your intelligence, your educational level, your thought processes, and your personality. Isn't it more important than selecting the right tie or handbag?

Sound Off: Elements of Voice

The elements of voice can be divided into three categories: vocal clarity, vocal variety, and vocal emphasis.

1. Vocal clarity consists of tone, pace, volume, and pitch. Speaking clearly enables listeners to understand what you are saying,
2. Vocal variety makes your voice interesting and engaging to the listener. Two skills that help with vocal variety are pitch and rate of speech.
3. Vocal emphasis lets the listeners know what you think is important and guides them to make the same judgment. It includes inflection and strategic pauses.

When used effectively and in combination, these skills help people deliver a message with poise, power, and passion. Your voice can make you stand out from other candidates, particularly those who mumble or speak in a monotone.

President Barack Obama is an excellent example of a speaker who speaks clearly, emphasizes words for impact, and infuses his warm personality into his speeches to make an emotional connection with his audiences.

Have you ever heard a parent reprimand a mouthy teenager by warning, "You'd better watch your tone of voice with me"? Or perhaps you were a rebellious teenager who was scolded in this way. Certainly, you are familiar with the expression "It's not what you say; it's how you say it." Your tone of voice plays a major role in communicating your message and expressing your emotions. Soft, murmuring tones are non-threatening and convey pleasure and bliss. Harsh, loud words convey displeasure and anger. Listen to your voice on a tape recorder and assess your own tone. Is it friendly or bland? Engaging or forgettable?

Ladies: Do you purr like a kitten with a soft, sensuous hum? Or do you squeal like an excitable junior high school girl? If you're lucky, your voice is controlled and melodious.

Men: Do you rumble like thunder, evoking an image of Darth Vader? Or do you talk a mile a minute like a slick used-car salesman? If you're blessed, you have a deep, resounding voice.

When your tone is clear, strong, and energetic, people naturally assume you are capable and confident. If your tone is soft and low, people may assume you are weak, timid, or just plain exhausted. If you use no inflection in your voice, you may be viewed as boring or unimaginative even if you are highly intelligent and creative.

Here are some ways to inject some life in your voice during an interview:

- Reveal your personality by emphasizing key words to add impact. If you were a hiring manager, you would warm up faster to someone who shows personality, rather than a bore.
- When telling an anecdote, relive the experience in your mind so you are more in the moment, and sound animated and excited about it. Don't go hog-wild, though, and act frantic. The result could leave a crazy bad impression on the interviewer.
- Use corresponding facial expressions or hand gestures to double the impact of your words.
- Vary your tone and pitch to make your speech pattern more interesting. A monotone will put listeners to sleep—as you experienced for yourself in those boring lectures in school.
- Speak loudly enough, so the interviewer does not need to strain to hear you, but not so loudly that the interviewer reaches for ear plugs.

Voice Modulation

You've heard the expression, "Moderation in everything." When it comes to using your voice for maximum impact, the operative phrase is "Modulation is everything." Modulation is simply varying the pitch of your voice rather than speaking in a monotone, which puts people to sleep faster than a sleeping pill. Modulation makes your voice more pleasing and interesting to the listener. Nearly everyone modulates their voice naturally in social situations, but often they are so nervous or overwhelmed when delivering a business speech or answering questions in a job interview that they forget to add some variety to their speech pattern.

You can practice modulating your voice by slowing the pace and enunciating clearly to emphasize a point. When summarizing a final and very important point, deliver it with a faster pace. Then, pause and repeat the last few words in a slower, lower voice. The different delivery styles will make the point stand out.

Open Wide

Do you talk through your nose? If you do, people probably have remarked that you sound nasal. That's too bad because many people find a nasal tone demanding and calculating. You can overcome the nasal sound by opening your mouth more as you talk. This action encourages the sound waves to emanate from your voice box, not through your nose.

Perfect Your Pitch

Women typically have higher pitched voices than men. Women with high, squeaky voices sound irritating and are perceived to be immature and inexperienced while those with low-pitched voices may be viewed as unfeminine, or downright masculine. When you speak quickly, the pitch rises. Thus, women who already have high voices should slow down a bit. If you are a squeaker, don't fret. You can work with a vocal coach to lower your pitch slightly and sound less annoying.

A clear and confident voice is an essential business skill, especially for men. Effective leaders, managers, and communicators usually have deep, low voices which give them an authoritative presence. A deep voice exudes strength because it a sign of high testosterone, and it commands more attention than a fast, squeaky voice. That is why men with deep voices are often found in high positions.

Pace Yourself

The speed of your speech is an important aspect in communication. You can pick up the pace to add energy and animation to your voice. Speeding up will invariably make the tone of voice more urgent or compelling, but if you speak too quickly, you may appear nervous, and your speech could be difficult to understand.

You should slow your speech down to emphasize important points and allow time for the listener to absorb the information. Try to control your speech without slowing it down too much. Speech that is too slow is monotonous and boring.

Pleasing Pauses

Silence is an excellent exclamation point. By slightly extending a pause, you can emphasize a key point, concept, or anecdote. If you're stuck for an answer, you can pause and say, "That's a good question." It signals to the interviewer that you need a moment to compose your response. If you pause too often, however, you will look unprepared, so keep your pauses to a minimum for maximum impact.

Don't Fill 'er Up

Beware of using fillers or padding in your speech. Fillers are sounds and words that have no meaning but are used to keep a person's speech flowing. Some of the most commonly used fillers are "er," "um," "uh," "you know," and "all righty." These words serve as padding but also give the interview the impression that you lack confidence or, even worse, you don't know what you're talking about. Speaking fluidly without these annoying little distractions will give you a confident air of authority. It pays to sound like a professional in high-stakes interviewing.

Practice Perfectly

In an interview, you must come across as polished, confident, and natural. You can achieve this level of natural confidence by rehearsing your responses to potential interview questions until you can say the answers effortlessly. By saying the responses aloud, you will be more prepared when it's show time.

Ask a friend to role play with you, so you can rehearse your responses using different speeds, pitches, and volumes to determine the most effective combination for driving home key points. You can ask your friend to videotape you, and then you will be able to critique your vocals and accompanying facial expressions and gestures.

Cures for Cotton Mouth

It is completely normal to feel tense before you walk into a job interview, particularly if you have been searching for a job for a while. After all, this is your big chance, and you want to create a good impression. Fortunately, there are some common-sense cures to prevent or alleviate dry mouth, a crackly voice, or a case of the nerves, so you'll come across as cool and collected even if you're not.

Drink water: Before your interview, drink a glass of water to moisten your vocal chords. Why do you think Letterman and Leno keep water pitchers on their desks?

Breathe: Practice deep abdominal breathing before your interview. Fully inhale and exhale. This method will calm your nerves and give you a sense of stability before your interview.

Put the candy bar away: Eating a chocolate bar before your interview will make your throat feel scratchy.

Ditch the dairy: Milk and other dairy products lead to mucous formation. You wouldn't want to hock a loogie during your interview.

Lay off the hot stuff: Spicy food can cause acid reflux, not to mention bad breath. Spare the interviewer.

The Way You Talk

It is important to appear professional in an interview, so you must avoid slang and colloquialisms, such as "you know." In everyday life, you may have picked up some bad speaking habits that can negatively impact your interviewer's impression of you. If you hale from various parts of the United States, you might talk like a Valley Girl, a redneck, or a gangsta.

In such a case, you will need to practice your pronunciation, enunciation, and rhetoric before walking into an interview.

Rate the Behavior

For this exercise, use the Psychotron to rate the following speech patterns below from crazy bad to crazy bad-ass.

Talk Like a Valley Girl

Some Gen X and Gen Y females have adopted the Valley Girl way of speaking. This style of speech, which originated in California's San Fernando Valley and was made popular in the movie *Clueless*, occurs nationwide. You should seek treatment if you exhibit any of the following speech patterns:

- You speak with a high rising terminal. That means your sentences end with a rising intonation as if you are asking a question with every statement you make.
- You say the word "like" at least once in every sentence; for example, "She like aced her LSATs, and like, got into law school right away."
- You use the words "totally" or "way" in place of "very" or "really." For example, "I could totally do this job. It's way cool."
- You add the word "duh" or "whatever" to any negative statement (with a slight pause between what and ever). "I was fired from my last job for being late. Whatever."
- In place of "good" or "great", you use these words: "awesome," "amazing," "rad," "sweet," "classic," "excellent." "You know, like, I could totally see myself in this job. It sounds amazing."

Talk Like a Redneck

Redneck humor, also called blue-collar comedy, has experienced a surge in popularity. Heck, there's even a redneck comedy channel. The term redneck refers to a distinct class of people who live in rural areas of the United States. When used by outsiders, the word can be insulting, but many rednecks are proud to call themselves rednecks.

Are you a redneck? If you talk loudly, like to cuss, and are comfortable with the phrases below, you just might be one. Kick it up a notch when you are interviewing by enunciating your words, unless the interviewer is a redneck. In that case, the two of you will be in hog heaven.

BAHS (noun). A supervisor.
FARD (verb). Fired.
Usage: "My bahs done fard me for reading huntin' magazines at work."
UHMERKIN (noun). A person who lives in the United States of Uhmerka.
PURD (adjective). Proud.
Usage: "I'm purd to be a Uhmerkin."
SINNER (noun). Exact middle of.
Usage: "I wanna work at the new shoppin' sinner."
RETAR (verb). To stop working.
Usage: "I wanna retar when I'm 65."
JAW-JUH (noun). State north of Florida.
Usage: "I went to school in Jaw-juh."
AST (verb). To interrogate or inquire.
Usage: "The interviewer ast lots of hard questions."

Talk Like a Gangsta

Rap is still popular, along with wearing sagged pants and walking like a gangsta, but it's totally inappropriate for a job interview. Gangsta talk is a cool version of redneck talk, and is indicative of today's youth culture. If any of the following phrases are part of your everyday speech, leave them at home before you venture out on a job interview. You'll be considered annoying and disrespectful if you talk like a gangsta when face-to-face with the interviewer.

- Instead of saying "For sure," you say "fo sho" (the last letters are silent)
- "I is fro da street o L.A." (or Chicago, New York, or Philly).
- When greeting the interviewer or hiring manager, your first inclination is to say "Yo," "Sup," or "Wazzup."
- You say, "You know," "Ya dig," or "Know what I'm sayin."
- You use the following expressions: "Don't be trippin," "Don't be hatin," "Break yo' self," or "Don't be bustin' my chops."

(Caution: If you mispronounce any of these phrases when you're in the 'hood, you may be "dissed when yo chillin' wit yo homies." Translation: This lingo is cool—and expected—when you're hanging out with your friends, but it's the kiss of death in a job interview.)

Employers want to hire job candidates who are good communicators, so even if you don't talk like a Valley Girl, a redneck, or a gangster, be cognizant of your grammar usage and enunciate your words clearly during a job interview.

PART III

ACT Out: Thank

14 | After the Interview: Thank 'em Like Crazy

You have just concluded a highly anticipated job interview. You prepared for it very diligently and tried to use every golden nugget that you ever read on successful job interviewing. The hiring manager has just escorted you out of the conference room and down the hallway to the elevator. Your mind is racing with a million questions as you leave the building. Did you make a good impression? Did you say all the right things? Did you convince the interviewer that you are the right fit for the job and the organization's culture?

Do not make the assumption that your hard work in preparing for the interview is over, and all you have to do now is sit and wait. You have more work cut out for you. This chapter is about thanking your interviewer(s) and following up with the organization, which is the third stage of the ACT Out interview process. You must keep the communication ball rolling with your potential employer after the interview to maximize your chances of landing the job.

The Waiting Game

After reflecting briefly on the interview, your initial reaction is that everything went reasonably well. You put into practice everything you learned in this book to set yourself apart—in a crazy good way—from the other candidates under consideration. The employer would be insane not to offer you the job on a silver platter. But how do you handle a potential employer who plays the agonizing waiting game with you? Mind you, the decision makers are not sadists who live for making you sweat and squirm even though it seems like it. You want to know if you got the job, and you want to know right now.

If you're impatient by nature, and you can't handle the pressure, there's an easy way to avoid all of the suspense: Just ask.

Some interviewers may be caught a bit off guard by your directness, but most will admire your assertiveness and sincere interest in understanding the next steps in the hiring process and where you stand among your competition. After all, your time is valuable, too.

You may be told that the company needs to meet with several other job candidates before conducting second interviews or making the final hiring decision. Instantly, you think, "Oh, no!" You were hoping the interviewer would cancel all other interviews after meeting you. After all, you have presented yourself as the best, the brightest, and the fairest in the land. The interviewer's search is over.

Don't worry yourself sick. The HR department might have some guidelines in place about interviewing a certain number of candidates.

More likely, the interviewer might be feeding you a line of bull to buy some time. The interviewer could be sold on you but needs to discuss the hiring decision with other people in the organization and check your references. There are so many variables to consider that it is senseless to venture a guess. Don't agonize over it. Put yourself out of your misery simply by inquiring about the hiring and decision-making process at the end of the interview.

Before the interviewer escorts you out of the conference room, it is appropriate to ask the following questions to set the stage for future contact:

- If you need more information about my job experience and qualifications, I can email it to you right away.
- I'd like to convey more job-related information in a second interview. Do you know when that will be?
- When will selected candidates be invited back to meet with other decision-makers?
- When will you make a hiring decision?
- By what date do you hope to fill the position?
- When can I expect a call from you, one way or another?
- Can I follow up with you next week if I don't hear anything?
- What is your preferred method of follow-up communication? I'd like to touch base again.

Good Signs

In Chapter 9, you learned that it's important to establish a rapport with your interviewer, who will be instrumental in advancing you to the next stage of the hiring process if you made a favorable impression. Many interviewers are skilled at putting on a poker face, like the lyrics in Lady GaGa's hit song of the same name, and you are left with a big question mark in your head. Eventually, they will give you an indication of what they think of you. But even if you strike a good rapport, it does not mean you will get the job simply because the interviewer seemed to like you, smiled, and laughed at your jokes.

Look for positive signs of good synergy. You're probably a shoo-in for the next round of interview if your interviewer exhibited some of the following behaviors:

- Showed interest by leaning toward you.
- Exhibited positive body language, such as sitting in an expansive position rather than a restricted position.
- Smiled occasionally and nodded his or her head in agreement.
- Put phone calls on hold.
- Established good eye contact and focused only on you, not on your necklace, your tie, or a picture on the wall.
- Exhibited some mirroring techniques.
- The interviewer talked up the benefits of the job and working for the company.

- Ran over the allotted interview time.
- Asked probing questions about your background to learn about your professional and personal aspirations.
- Made statements that indicated you are already an employee, such as "You will attend a weekly staff meeting . . ." or "When you fill out your timesheet . . . ."
- Inquired when you could start working.
- Handed you his or business card at the end of the interview.
- Discussed next steps in the interview process.
- Called your references right after the interview.

The Doctor Is In . . .

"Clean up your Facebook page. Delete racy photos or party pics, such as chugging beers or giving a middle-finger salute with your drunken pals. Employers will check you out thoroughly before extending a job offer."

Red Flags

Conversely, there are some obvious signs that your interview did not go well. When you cannot establish a connection with the interviewer and your communication is dead in the water, your chances do not look good. Did your experience any of the following crazy bad scenarios?

Fast and Furious

If your interview was cut short and the interviewer rushed you out of the office, you can chalk up another failed attempt. The interviewer immediately recognized that you were not a good fit or a viable candidate, and cut her losses quickly and painlessly. Her behavior is an extremely crazy bad sign if you were scheduled to meet with several people afterward.

Attention Deficit

If your interviewer started shuffling paperwork or answered her phone while you were talking, those are telltale signs that she was not remotely interested in what you had to say. She asked no clarifying questions about your answers, and her upper lip twitched as you babbled. Hopefully, you endured her rudeness, thanked her for her time, shook her hand, and left the room with a small shred of dignity. Of course, no one would blame you if you felt like giving her a piece of your mind a la Alex Forrest, the deranged stalker played by Glenn Close in the movie *Fatal Attraction* when she told Dan Gallagher played by Michael Douglas "I will not be ignored!"

However, you know what they say about burning your bridges: You cannot cross over them again. Do not do or say anything that you will later regret.

The Doctor Is In . . .

"It's always a bad sign when you bring out the interviewer's nervous tics. Be warm and confident, but don't come on too strong."

Drawing a Blank

The interviewer left you high and dry and wondering if you would be called back. There was no discussion of next steps or salary requirements. You could not even understand the interviewer's shrill last words as she ran out of the office and down the hallway trying to escape.

A Two-Timer

If you were invited back for a second interview, but no one showed you around the office or introduced you to other employees, you have good reason to wonder if you will receive an offer. Your prospective employer may still be deciding if you are a good fit and did not want you to start feeling at home.

Touching Base after the Interview

The job interview isn't finished until the paperwork is done. You must pay attention to your post-interview follow-up. This final step could increase your chances of getting a job offer over other candidates who ignore this vital part of the interview process. If the employer is on the fence about you, prompt follow-up could tip the odds in your favor. It shows respect for the interviewer, demonstrates good manners, and is indicative of the professionalism and attention to detail that you would bring to your job performance.

When crafting your letter, use the engineering principle called KISS, which is an acronym for *Keep It Simple, Sweetheart* or, depending on your mood, *Keep It Simple, Stupid.* It's a thank-you note, not an essay, so readers appreciate when you make your point quickly and succinctly. Keep it one page in length.

A formal thank-you letter serves as a valuable tool to market your talents to the employer. If you want the job, you will have to communicate your sentiments in a well-worded letter. Bottom line: It's suck up time. A follow-up letter will keep you at the top of the employer's mind, underscores your UVP, recaps relevant job qualifications, and conveys additional information that will help you garner favor. For example, if you are proficient in operating special machinery or using some cutting-edge software, now is the time to stress these competencies.

Be sure to ask for business cards, so the contact information will be at your fingertips when you compose your letters. You should mail or email a personalized thank-you letter to every person who interviewed you within 24 hours of the interview. Your letter should thank them for their time and reiterate your interest in joining the team. A typed letter on good-quality stationary or an email is appropriate. A handwritten note is warm and fuzzy but not as business-like.

A professional thank-you letter contains five main parts:

1. Salutation: Even if the interviewer asked you to call him or her by their first name, it is better to err on the side of caution and write: Dear Dr./Mr./Ms./Mrs. _____.
2. First paragraph: Thank the interviewer for his or her time, and for the opportunity to interview for the job. State the job position to refresh their memory. You should state your initial positive impressions about the company or organization.
3. Second paragraph: Recap your qualifications that make you the right candidate for the job and add pertinent job-related information that you

did not convey during the interview. If you learned about a problem or situation in the company that could benefit from your skills and experience, now is the time to address it and offer your services.

4. Last paragraph: Emphasize your continued interest in the job, working for the company, and your desire to be contacted about the hiring decision. Provide two or more ways for the interviewer to get in touch with you.

5. Signature: The following closings are appropriate: Sincerely, Yours truly, Respectfully, Regards, Kind Regards.

Before you mail or email a thank-you letter, use your computer's Spell Check function to ensure it is letter perfect. A letter filled with bad grammar and typos is as bad as no follow-up at all.

The Doctor Is In . . .

"If you were interviewed by a panel, it is not necessary to write individual letters to each person. Simply write and send one letter to the head interviewer, thanking the panel as a group within the body of the letter."

After you send your thank-you letter, you must sit tight and wait for the good or bad news. If more than a week passes, and you have not heard a peep, then you can call or email the employer to politely ask for an update. This action shows you are persistent and still interested in the job.

#1 Crazy Good Thank-You Letter

Dear Mr. Wilson:

Thank you for the privilege of interviewing with you yesterday during your recruiting visit to Michigan State University (MSU). The sales management training program you outlined sounds challenging, rewarding, and in alignment with my career objectives.

As I mentioned during the interview, I will graduate with a bachelor's degree in marketing in May. I was an intern for the past two summers at a marketing agency in Detroit, and I can provide you with excellent references attesting to my job performance and work ethic. I hope you will agree this internship is an excellent springboard into Acme Corporation's sales management training program.

I have a keen interest in working for your company. Per your request, I have enclosed my college transcript and a list of professional and personal references, along with contact information. I look forward to hearing from you. You can reach me at (313) 555-1234 or topcandidate@aol.com.

Sincerely,

Dennis Michaels

#2 Crazy Good Thank-You Letter

Dear Mr. Peepers:

It was a pleasure meeting you today to discuss the position of accounting specialist at ABC Company. I enjoyed learning about the responsibilities of the position and getting an overview of the company.

I am confident that my education, job experience, and skill sets would be assets in this role, and make me a significant contributor to the company's growth and bottom line. In particular, I believe my problem-solving skills would help in restructuring your accounting department, based on my success in rectifying a similar situation for my past employer. I would like to thank you for your time and reiterate my interest in working at ABC Company. I look forward to hearing from you regarding your hiring decision for this exciting career opportunity.

Regards,

Becky Johnson

467 Hillcrest Drive

Anytown, USA 60126

Tel: (312) 555-0137

Cell: (312) 555-8935

#3 Crazy Good Thank-You Letter

Harry Goliath

Brickwall Modular Construction Co.

333 Mortar Ave.

Anytown, FL 35332

Dear Mr. Goliath:

Thank you for the opportunity to interview for the position of associate architect at Brickwall Modular Construction Co. I am very interested and excited about the prospect of working in your design division.

In addition to my six years of experience in a similar role, I have great organizational skills, meticulous attention to detail, excellent communication skills, and I can interface well with people at all levels of an organization. This skill would be valuable in working with the employees in your manufacturing facility.

On a more personal note, I am interested in being part of your Habitat for Humanity initiative because I am passionate about helping others and making a difference in the world.

I look forward to hearing from you soon regarding the position of architect.

Respectfully,

Jeffrey Whitney

100 Pleasant Ave.

Anytown, USA 10000

Tel: (305) 555-8245

#1 Crazy Bad Thank-You Letter

Dear Tiffany,

I appreciate you taking time out of your busy day to meet with me about the IT manager position. I am recently divorced, and I think I would really enjoy working closely with you.

With 10 years of rock-solid experience, I would be a good addition to your IT department. I am committed to excellence and don't mind working long hours and weekends. I also have season tickets for the Lakers, if you ever want to catch a game with me. I wait in great anticipation of your hiring decision for the IT position. If you don't offer me the job, I hope you will still consider going to a Lakers game. I think you're hot.

Yours truly,

Paul Douchet

#2 Crazy Bad Thank-You Letter

Dear Mr. Bartholomew:

It was nice meeting you yesterday to discuss the bank job and tour your impressive, state-of-the-art facility. I have a wealth of experience that directly relates to the position of assistant bank manager, especially in the area of securing and transferring funds to Swiss banks.

In my free time, I shoot guns at a local target practice range. This skill might come in handy if there's a robbery at your bank. In closing, I would be delighted to hear from you and also learn more about your bank's new security system.

Ciao!

Vito Scallopini

#3 Crazy Bad Thank-You Letter

Dear Mr. Johnson:

Thanks for interviewing me the other day for the sales manager opening at your retail store in Milwaukee.

My retail background is an ideal match for the job requirements you outlined in our discussion. I feel I would do an excellent job because I am familiar with all aspects of store management, and I am dedicated to providing top-notch customer service.

I cannot help remarking that you bear a strong resemblance to my beloved grandfather, who passed away last year. A lovely urn on my fireplace mantel holds his ashes, and I speak to his spirit daily.

I look forward to your response regarding the sales manager position. If hired, I can start immediately. My references are enclosed, per your request. You can reach me at (818) 555-7722 or keepthefaith@aol.com.

Sincerely,

Miriam Goodheart

P.S.: Enclosed is my favorite photo of "Poppy."

Crazy Bad Follow-Up Efforts

Some candidates go over the top in trying to get noticed in their follow-up communications. Even if you have a flair for the dramatic, it is not professional to send singing telegrams, flowers, cookies, balloons, or other gimmicks that call unfavorable attention to yourself.

It should go without say that the following behaviors are inappropriate:

- Stalking the interviewer.
- Showing up at the office repeatedly.
- Lurking in the lobby or parking lot.
- Sending daily emails.
- Leaving continuous voice mails.
- Contacting him or her on Facebook.
- Writing threatening or just plain creepy letters.
- Promising sexual favors in exchange for employment. (Note: Nasty behavior could have a negative impact on your reputation and your career goals.)

There are always exceptions to the rule. Persistence can pay off if you are nonthreatening and take a low-key approach as shown in the following example.

Reappearing Act

A marketing director needed to hire a sales agent. He explained to each candidate that he was going to interview a lot of people before making a hiring decision. The first interviewee had all the right stuff. His job experience was well suited for the position, and he met all of the necessary requirements. But the marketing director did not want to hire the first candidate, and insisted on interviewing more people.

The first interviewee stopped by the office once a week for the next three weeks just to say hello and ask if the marketing director had made a decision yet. In many cases, this guy would have been viewed as a pest and sent away. But he was engaging and likeable, and not the least bit pushy.

Real-life result: The marketing director was impressed with the young man's persistence and finally offered him the job. He's been performing like a rock star in his role, delivering great results, and is well-liked by the entire staff.

15

Post-Interview Self-Evaluation: How Did You Do?

How do you feel about the way you conducted yourself in your important one-on-one meeting? Were you poised and confident under pressure because you implemented all of the advice in the last 14 chapters of this book? Now that it's over, are you excited and exuberant? Or deflated and defeated? Do you feel hopeful, or are you sick to your stomach?

You would not be human if you didn't replay the entire episode in your head over and over again, from the time you were introduced to the interviewer, shook hands, and were invited to take a seat, until you rose from the chair 30 minutes or an hour later, shook his hand again, and thanked him for his time and the opportunity to interview for the available position. In the allotted time period, you applied the information you learned in this book. You stated your unique value proposition (UVP) as it applies to the job in question, your five-sentence life history, your three key strengths, and other relevant information about your background and life experiences. You're pleased with some of your responses to the interviewer's questions, and not so pleased with other answers. Don't keep kicking yourself in the head. We have all been there. Hopefully, you'll learn a few lessons

197

that will work to your benefit in your next interview if you don't snag this job.

The best time to evaluate your interview performance is when your gut feeling is still present (hopefully, it's not aching and gnawing at you) within a few hours of the interview when even the most minute details are still fresh in your mind. Some job seekers find it helpful to create a self-evaluation tool, so they can rate their post-interview performance immediately. This is also part of this interview strategy stage as you will take stock on your own feelings and reactions to your interview performance, assess ways to make improvements, and be introspective and realistic about your career goals and aspirations as they relate to the jobs you are interviewing for.

Rate Yourself; Don't Berate Yourself

You should approach every interview as a learning experience that has some key takeaways. By making a few notes, you will able to identify factors that lead to a weak or a strong performance, correct your mistakes, improve your responses, and perform better overall in future interviews.

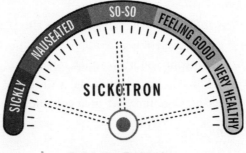

Rate the Behavior

For the following self-evaluation exercise, you will rate yourself on the Sickotron, a version of the Psychotron that gauges your physical reaction to your interview performance. The rating categories are:

- Healthy: I aced it and I feel great.
- Feeling good: I felt good overall.
- So-So: I felt okay, but I need more practice.

- Nauseated: My performance made me ill. Get me a barf bag.
- Sickly: Call an ambulance. I almost died in there.

Interview Preparation

1. Did you arrive on time for the interview?
2. Were you appropriately attired for the interview?
3. Did you bring the right materials and samples with you?
4. Did you research the company in advance and check out the website, annual report, and other pertinent information?
5. Did you prepare your unique value proposition (UVP) as it relates to the job?
6. Did you prepare three to five thoughtful questions to ask at the end of the interview?
7. Did you feel well prepared to answer the interviewer's questions?

Nonverbal Communication

8. Did you give the interviewer a firm handshake when introduced?
9. Did you maintain good eye contact?
10. Did you sit straight and squarely in the chair in the "tell" position?
11. Did you squirm in your chair trying to get into a comfortable position?
12. Were you relaxed and in control throughout the interview?
13. Did you use gestures to emphasize important points?
14. Did you fidget with your hands?
15. Did you exhibit enthusiasm?
16. Did you use mirroring techniques during the interview?
17. Did you establish a connection with the interviewer?
18. Did your facial expressions match your content?

Verbal Communication

19. Did you speak clearly and eloquently?
20. Did you talk too much?
21. Did you talk too little?
22. Did you pause before stating key points?
23. Did you avoid using padding, such as "you know," "er," and "um"?
24. Did you refrain from using slang or talking like a Valley Girl, a redneck, or a gangsta?
25. Did you keep any generational differences in mind to enhance your communication with the interviewer?

Interview Content Matter

26. Name three things that you did well in the interview.
27. Name three things that you would change or improve.
28. Did you state your unique value proposition (UVP)?
29. Did you relate your transferable skills to the job?
30. Did you articulate relevant skills and accomplishments?
31. What questions did you ace?
32. What questions were difficult to answer?
33. If you could answer the difficult questions again, how would you respond?
34. What skills and qualifications seemed to interest the hiring manager the most?
35. Is there any information that you would research more deeply before the interview?
36. Were your responses consistent with the information on your resume?
37. Did you back up your answers with supporting evidence or anecdotes?
38. Did you ask questions about the job or the company that indicate you did your homework?
39. Do you feel that you convinced the interviewer that you are the best candidate for the job?

Parting Shots

40. Did you reiterate your interest in the job at the end of the interview?
41. Did you ask the interviewer about next steps in the hiring process?
42. Did you shake hands at the end of the interview?
43. How would you rate your interview performance on the Sickotron?

Follow-Up Communications

44. Did you send a thank-you letter to your interviewer(s) within 24 hours?
45. Did you make sure the interviewer has all of your contact information (phone, cell, email)?
46. Did you send any additional information or samples that were requested?

How do you think you scored with the interviewer? If there are any sections in the self-evaluation where you think you can use some improvement, get at it. Ask a friend or a trusted colleague to role play with you and videotape your mock interviews. Watch the video and be objective when critiquing your performance. Invite constructive feedback from your friends and family members. Keep practicing until you are satisfied with your performance and are confident that you will shine in your next interview. Your goal is to leave the interview feeling energized and invigorated, not like you want to duck into the nearest restroom and throw up.

A Win-Win Result

If you receive a phone call the very next day—or sooner—it's a sign that you aced the interview. The company wants to schedule a second interview or extend a job offer before you have an opportunity to interview elsewhere. In this case, they are very excited about you. Congratulations. Whether this a bona fide job offer or a call back to schedule a second interview, you obviously did something right.

Close, But No Cigar

The expression "Close, but no cigar" dates back to the mid-twentieth century when county fairground game booths awarded cigars as prizes. The phrase means to fall short of a successful outcome and receive nothing for your efforts. The phrase can apply to interviewing for a job and being oh-so-close to getting an offer, but—for some strange and mystical reason—you were not the lucky winner. (Note: when other people receive job offers, it is pure luck. When you receive an offer, it's because you impressed the employer with your outstanding credentials, wit, and charm.)

Even if you dazzled the interviewer(s) with your straight posture, good eye contact, firm handshake, enthusiasm, clear and commanding voice, stellar academic record and qualifications, and spot-on responses to every question, you did not get a callback or a job offer. So, what went wrong?

If you receive a phone call with bad news, it is the ideal opportunity to ask for specific advice on how you can improve your performance or make a better impression. If you receive similar feedback from two or more interviewers, consider yourself fortunate. You have identified your problem area(s) and can start making positive changes.

While you have the interviewer on the phone, make the most of it by asking if there are any other open positions in the organization. Do not assume that losing out on one job means that you have no chance of working for that employer ever again. It pays to be gracious, courteous, and reiterate your interest in working for the company. Who knows? The selected candidate may not work out, and you might be next in line to be contacted with a job offer.

If the bad news arrives via email, reply within 24 hours with a thank-you letter and ask what you could have done to improve your interview performance. Many people do not mind responding to a request for constructive criticism as long as you seem sincere about improving yourself.

If a third party, such as a headhunter or a recruiter, arranged the interview for you, the employer may tell them why you were not hired. Chances are that this third party will contact you immediately to convey this information.

Even if you receive a rejection letter, you should always send a thank-you letter to show you are a good sport. This gesture of professionalism may even cement you in the interviewer's mind when another position becomes available.

Do You *Really* Want to Work There?

You have been so wrapped up worrying if the potential employer liked you that you forgot to consider your own feelings. If you have been eating beans every night for a few months, dumpster diving, reading by candlelight, and selling off your possessions at yard sales to pay bills, then it would be wise for you to accept any job offer that comes your way. However, if you're in a position to be more selective, there are many factors to consider before you accept an offer and end your job search. A new full-time job is a commitment, and, like marriage, is for better or worse. It is difficult to interview for jobs when you are tied down to the 8-to-5 daily grind.

Is it an organization where you can grow, learn new skills, and build a career? Would you feel comfortable working in the organization's culture and environment? In today's economy, it's not unusual for a company to be doing well one day and then close its doors the next, leaving countless employees without a job and a paycheck. If hired, is there job security?

The old expression is worth its weight in gold: A bird in the hand is worth two in the bush.

Translation: Do not give up a secure job for a shiny new one that promises more money and perks if you have any hesitations at all.

If your new employer is on shaky financial ground, you could quickly become a casualty and find yourself collecting unemployment compensation and vying for a low-paying job, along with many other over-qualified candidates. If the company seems solid, but the job does not align with your career goals, you can accept it and keep your eyes open for the right job to come along. In the meantime, you are employed and putting food on the table. Take some quiet time to think through the ramifications of accepting a job offer, how it matches your worldview (Chapter 7) and how it will affect all aspects of your life.

The following signs are good indications that the company is prospering:

1. It is investing in its leadership.
2. Employees have worked there a long time.
3. It is on solid financial ground.
4. Its products and services are in demand.
5. It wins awards for product design, customer service, sales revenue, and other indicators.

In contrast, keep your eyes peeled for these signs that a prospective employer is going to bite the bullet:

1. There is rapid employee turnover.
2. The company has a bad credit history.
3. The company reputation in the community or in the industry is questionable.
4. Executives start unloading their stock.
5. The company is selling major assets, such as well-performing divisions or capital goods, for short-term survival.
6. Surprise visits from off-site attorneys, accountants, auditors, and other circling vultures signal imminent danger.

Generally, employers will give you a couple of days to mull over an offer. If you receive a phone call in less than 24 hours, it's a good sign that you aced it. The company wants dibs on you before you have an opportunity to interview elsewhere or consider other job offers.

So, get out your pencil and paper and make your Ben Franklin list of pros and cons. Simply draw a T with pros on the left side, and cons on the right. When you are done making your lists, the side with the most entries reflects the obvious decision.

What further information do you need about the company before you will accept a job offer? Is the company well known and well respected with name recognition that would be advantageous to your resume? Would this particular position help you achieve your long-term career goals? Does it require working long hours and weekends? If you're family-oriented, a demanding work schedule may wreak havoc on your home life. Would you receive an increase or a decrease in pay? Is it work you would thoroughly enjoy? How long is the commute? Is the total rewards package (compensation and benefits) satisfactory? Are there opportunities for professional development? How much travel, if any, is required?

Moral Dilemmas

What should you do if you receive a job offer from an employer who is rumored to be unethical? It depends on your circumstances but my rule of thumb is: Don't take it. You have heard the phrase "guilt by association." In the future, you will be judged by your employer's reputation, so it isn't worth it in the long term.

In Chapter 7, you read about worldviews and how you can apply them to decisions in all areas of your life. If you know what is important to you, you will have the confidence in your abilities and in yourself to steer clear from shady organizations.

16

Putting It All Together in a Crazy Good Way

Employers have a veritable toolkit of interview formats and techniques at their disposal to ensure they select the right candidates for available positions in their organizations, and more methods are being added all the time. Although the unique combination of your education, professional experience, and skills will get your foot in the door, it does not guarantee you a job offer.

Employers do not make hiring decisions based on merit alone; they are looking for the total package. Personality, confidence, enthusiasm, a positive attitude, and excellent interpersonal and communication skills count heavily in the selection process. In fact, a study by the Society of Human Resources Management (SHRM) proved this point when it showed that a candidate's background and qualifications were far less influential in hiring decisions than their professionalism and interview performance.

The job interview process itself continues to change with technological advances. In the not-too-distant past, job seekers enclosed their carefully worded letters of introduction and accompanying resumes, printed on high-quality Vellum stationery, in a stamped envelope and mailed them via

U.S. mail in response to an ad in the local newspaper. Then, they waited nervously by the phone in the hopes of receiving a call from a secretary to schedule a face-to-face, one-on-one interview with a hiring manager at the employer's jobsite.

Today, job seekers take a different approach to snagging an interview. Potential candidates email their letters of introduction with a resume attachment in response to an ad posted on an employer's website, Craigslist, Monster, or a plethora of other job sites. In turn, they may receive an auto-response confirming receipt of the email, or a personal email from a human resources manager to schedule a screening interview via phone or Skype.

Not only has communication changed based on new technology, the interview structure has been revamped. You could be asked situational questions, in which your responses are predictors of your behaviors, or you may be asked to recall past examples of how you performed in your previous jobs in the areas of team leadership, problem resolution, or employee conflict. You could be assessed quantitatively against other candidates, or be asked to make a presentation in front of a group of interviewers, as in the case of Heidi Bressler, a past finalist in *The Apprentice*, whose experience is detailed in Chapter 10.

Some organizations use mini-interviews in which five to eight interviewers are each assigned an area to assess in eight minutes or less. When the job interviewee completes one interview, off he goes to the next one. It's short, fast, and focused, like playing musical chairs.

In behavior-based interviews, you will be asked to share real-life experiences to illustrate your leadership, communications skills, and other traits. The questions segue from "Tell me what makes a great leader" to "Describe two situations where you demonstrated great leadership skills."

In another type of interview, you might be thrown into a fish bowl. You will take a seat at the conference table among four or five other interviewees, and a facilitator/interviewer will assign a group task. While the job candidates are busily working together on the task, evaluators are seated behind them to observe the group dynamics. Upon completion of the task, the facilitator will ask the group some difficult questions. Then, the candidates are evaluated on their behavior individually and as part of the group.

You may encounter all kinds of interviewers. Don't be fooled by those who appear too kind or too hardened. Often, the people who are smiling and nodding their heads in agreement are really barracudas, and those who look the most stoic are the friendliest and most willing to give you a chance. You need not figure them out; simply speak their generational language, use crazy good verbal and nonverbal communication skills to convey your relevant information effectively, and focus on your own performance. Not everyone is going to love you, but someone will.

So how can you stay ahead of new and different ways of being interviewed? By using the principles discussed in *Crazy Good Interviewing*.

Many of the behaviors and methods presented in this book are proven staples of good interviewing, such as a firm handshake, good eye contact, and a pleasant smile. When you combine these three elements, you set a positive tone for the interview and can build a strong rapport with the interviewer. This is easy stuff that many applicants forget when they are feeling overanxious. A little nervousness is good because it keeps you on your toes as you strive to make a good impression. A little overconfidence is good, too, as you will appear self-assured of your capabilities and what you bring to the employer's table.

Some people feel comfortable going into a job interview; others feel panicked to the point of nausea. Some applicants are ready to shine, and others fear the interviewer will judge them unfairly. Job candidates who attempt to memorize responses to typical questions will have the roughest time if their minds draw a blank, while those who can recall key bullet points will be primed and ready to answer questions more easily. This is just one of the many crazy good interview strategies that will help you sail through a job interview in a relaxed and effective manner, and make you feel good about your time in the interview office. If you invest time in practicing your interview strategies, behaviors, body language, and responses to oft-asked questions, you will be prepared for the expected—and the unexpected—and you could land a job offer.

Establish Your Power Base

When the interviewer invites you to have a seat, tell yourself that the chair will be your workplace for the next 10 minutes to one hour. Get yourself seated, situated, and comfortable. This is your home base from which you will make strong and lasting first impressions. Before you sit down, make sure your head is clear, and you do not sit in the chair behind the interviewer's desk by mistake. The best response to this faux pas is "I just wanted to get a feel for what it would be like to sit in this chair 10 years from now." Then smile, move to another chair, and proceed with the interview like nothing happened. The interviewer will admire your ability to recover from your error quickly and with humor.

As you wait in anticipation for the interviewer to begin firing away, you should feel secure that you have learned these key takeaways from *Crazy Good Interviewing*.

Use a Crazy Good Interview Strategy

Having a plan and knowing what you want to share with the interviewer will put you way ahead of the game. Your plan must include three key traits that you will bring to the position and three concrete examples of how you have used those traits in the past. Tie your past experiences and success stories to the position to illustrate your relevancy.

When it comes to discussing your skills, do not make the mistake of telling instead of showing. Use concrete examples to demonstrate your skills; for example, if you are skilled at successfully handling multiple tasks simultaneously, provide an example to paint a picture for the interviewer. This visual gives the interviewer something to remember after the interview, and helps him or her remember you when it comes time to make a hiring decision.

Use Crazy Good Behaviors to Get the Job

The anecdotes throughout this book illustrate how job applicants who displayed crazy good behaviors aced their interviews, while those who used crazy bad behaviors bombed, sometimes miserably. How can you modify and adapt these crazy good behaviors, so you can be successful in your own interview experiences while avoiding crazy bad behaviors that will be detrimental to your performance? Avoiding crazy bad behaviors—such as texting, answering your cell phone, yawning, or belching—won't guarantee you a job offer, but it will keep you in the running.

Sell Yourself Like Crazy

Highlight your unique value proposition (UVP), your top three strengths, and past professional and personal accomplishments. Back up your experience with a few memorable anecdotes that relate to the position. Infuse energy into your dialogue with appropriate hand gestures, facial expressions, and voice inflections to emphasize key points and make your interview come alive. If you are not excited about your candidacy, the interviewer won't be either.

Be Yourself, in a Crazy Good Way

A common mistake that many candidates make is not being authentic. They feel they must don a mask and play a role that fits a certain mold. To their dismay, this strategy is destined to backfire. You will be surprised how easy it is to detect insincerity during an interview, and it will only hurt you and the employer in the end when you reveal your true personality.

In Chapter 10, a former Vice President of Talent and Culture said she can spot a phony a mile away, and a Regional Marketing Director hired a candidate partly because he was so impressed by his genuineness. Thus, it pays to be sincere and honest while staying focused on how you can provide value in the position and be an asset to the organization. Demonstrate your true uniqueness by relating stories about your job experiences and tying them to the position.

Research the Employer Like Crazy

One of the best job interview strategies that most candidates ignore is to study the company's current events, so you can ask pertinent questions. This clearly shows the interviewer that you have done your homework, and you have a genuine interest in the company. Knowing as much as you can about the organization will give you a leg up against your competition, as shown in the following crazy good interview story.

Rate the Behavior

Using the Psychotron, how would rate the job candidate's behavior described in the following real-life interview?

More than Skin Deep

The Vice President of Marketing of a major manufacturer in the health and beauty care industry was trying to fill a slot for a Director of Marketing. He was looking for someone who would blow his socks off in the interview. When he met a well-dressed executive type, he knew he had found his man.

The candidate had gone above and beyond in doing his homework on the company—he had thoroughly researched its line of skin care products, its industry competitors, and the industry overall. His probing and relevant questions absolutely knocked the VP out of his chair because they were so insightful. The job candidate turned the interview dynamic around to position himself as the buyer in the interview, and the VP was the seller. The candidate started off his questions with the following comments:

1. I read your annual report, and I understand that you have a problem in the area of research and development. How are you dealing with it?
2. A competitor has developed and introduced a new teen-age acne cream that is more advanced than your leading product. Do you feel threatened by your competitor's new product? What plans to you have for improving your product?

3. Your competitor is focusing its entire advertising campaign on a special ingredient in its new acne cream. Are you investigating the harmful potential side effects of this ingredient? Do you have plans to add this ingredient to your cream?

4. Did you know that you have problems with your customer service department? I called the 800 number several times, and I did not have a pleasant experience. In some cases, I waited a long time for the call to be answered, I was put on hold immediately, or I was transferred to multiple parties without receiving any satisfactory responses.

5. Have you thought about restructuring the organization? I have some ideas I would like to share with you.

Real-life result: The Vice President of Marketing was completely sold on the candidate, primarily because of his in-depth questions. The candidate accepted the job offer and has received many accolades for his top performance.

Research the Interviewer(s) Like Crazy

If you know your interviewer's name, you can uncover professional and personal information by doing a Google search or checking out his or her Facebook and LinkedIn pages. By finding some common ground—such as graduating from the same university, belonging to the same professional organization, or volunteering for the same charitable organizations—you can make an immediate connection, establish a rapport, and increase your chances of advancing to the next stage in the interview process.

This strategy worked beautifully for a high-level university administrator who was pursuing a high-stakes position. She found out everything she could about her interviewers on the Internet. In the end, she received the job offer because, as one interviewer said, "She knows more about us than we do."

(Note: Be subtle when you raise interesting points about the interviewer's background. If you are very direct and appear to know too much professional and personal information, you may look like a stalker—which is not only crazy bad behavior, it's crazy scary.)

Practice Like Crazy

Seneca, a first-century Roman philosopher, allegedly said, "Luck is where the crossroads of opportunity and preparation meet." How true. If you practice your responses to interview questions in advance—like the ones in the Appendix of this book—you can gain an edge against other job candidates.

Ask a friend or a family member to do some mock interviews with you and record or videotape your practice runs. If you know someone who has real-life experience in interviewing and hiring employees, that is even better. With lots of practice and focus on the questions being asked, you will be able to uncover what is behind each question and be able to answer some of the unasked questions.

The Doctor Is In . . .

"You can improve your interview skills by videotaping mock interviews, and then watching them to identify areas that could use some work. First, pay attention to your nonverbal behavior. Then, pay attention to what you said. Finally, pay attention to how you said it. Keep practicing until you are satisfied with your performance."

Making it past the first round of interviews will give you a sense of satisfaction and put you one step closer to getting a job offer. The final interview is your last opportunity to impress interviewers with your UVP and top-notch communication and interpersonal skills, and position yourself as the lead candidate for the position. The initial interviews indicated how the company interviews and the type of individual desired to fill the position. At this point, you cannot sit back and relax. You must continually prepare and practice for the final interview, which will entail more in-depth questioning with the hiring manager or a panel of interviewers.

Take the Stage

A job interview is like opening night at the theater or a concert hall. The lights dim, the spotlight shines, and the performer must make an immediate connection with the audience. It is time to deliver and show what you've got. You gesture. You project. You bring crazy good energy to the room. Interviewing is the same way.

If your interviewing techniques are mediocre, or if you are sorely out of practice, you know what it feels like to interview your heart out only to be met with stony stares and rude remarks such as "Next," or "Don't call us; we'll call you." You blew your big chance, and a proverbial hooked cane appears out of nowhere and pulls you off stage—or out of the interviewer's office, in this case.

Luckily, now that scenario is a thing of the past. You have read this book from cover to cover, so you know crazy good interviewing behaviors like the palm of your hand. You can brush up on areas that can use some improvement. You can refer to this book for inspiration before you go on an interview. Your mantra should be: prepare, rehearse, and practice.

This book arms you with crazy good strategies, behaviors, and techniques to make a connection, create a favorable impression, and handle the toughest interviewers. Circling back to the singing analogy in Chapter 1, with practice you will be able to interview for a high-stakes position in front of complete strangers with little or no lead time, like the seasoned Karaoke singers who can take the stage, with a microphone in hand, to imitate the vocal stylings of Tony Bennett, Michael Bublé, Christina Aguilera, Seal, and Lady Gaga. You might discover that you enjoy interviewing, and basking in the afterglow of the interviewer's applause and whistles from HR directors chanting, "You're hired!"

The Doctor Is Out!

Appendix
150 Frequently
Asked Questions

Opening Remarks and Comments

Interviewers often engage in small talk to try to relax job candidates. When they sense you are ready to proceed, the real interview will commence. Start your engines. These examples signal that the interview has officially started.

1. "We are here today to gather more information about your work experiences, to learn about the skills you will bring to the position, and to gain insight about you as a person. We will share this information with our selection committee to determine if this position is a good fit for you and for us. We will have about 30 minutes together. At the end of the interview, I will give you an opportunity to ask any questions you might have. Here is my first question . . . ."

2. "I am going to ask you questions that will help us evaluate your credentials for this job and help you elaborate on what you submitted in your application. We will try to do this in the next 20 minutes."

3. "In the next 30 minutes, I will ask you a series of questions, so we can get to know each other better. Do you have any questions before we begin?"

4. "During the next 10 minutes, we will talk, so I can get to know you better, and you can get to know me. I will pass along this

information to the HR Director in the coming days. Do you mind
if I take notes? Here is your first question . . . ."

5. "Let's get started. In the next 40 minutes, we are going to talk
   about your past work experiences, your motivation for pursuing this
   position, and your interest in our organization."

Old-Time Favorite Questions

Here are some classic oldies but goodies that interviewers still use today to
begin or end an interview.

6. Tell me about yourself.
7. How would you describe yourself? (The alternate forms sound like
   this: How would others describe you? How would your friends
   describe you? How would your co-workers describe you?)
8. Why are you interested in this position? (An alternative is: Why are
   you applying to this position?)
9. Describe an ideal job and/or work environment.
10. What will you bring to this job and to this organization?
11. What can we tell you about this position to determine if this is a
    good fit for you?
12. What can we tell you about this position to get you to accept our
    offer?
13. How does this position fit into your long-range plans?
14. What are your strengths and weaknesses?
15. What is one area you would like to improve about yourself?
16. Where do you see yourself in 5 to 10 years career-wise?
17. How does this job align with your career plans?

Motivation Questions

Interviewers will ask the following questions to learn what motivates you
and gets your motor running.

18. In general, what motivates you in the workplace to get the job done?
19. If you could identify one driving force that underlies everything you
    do, what would it be?

20. What is the source of your driving force?
21. How does your driving force help you?
22. What three factors are motivating you to pursue this position at this point in your life?
23. Why is this the right time for you to pursue this job?
24. If you had to choose a reason for pursuing this job, which of the following applies?
    A. Greater responsibility
    B. Increase in money and power
    C. Career advancement
25. Tell me about a time when you encountered an obstacle and what you did to overcome it.
26. Tell me about a time when you lacked motivation for a project.
27. How did you resolve your lack of motivation?
28. Describe your proudest personal accomplishment.
29. Describe your proudest professional accomplishment.
30. What motivated you to pursue your proudest personal and professional endeavors?
31. How do you see your career developing over the next 5 to 10 years?
32. How will you achieve your 5- and 10-year career goals?
33. What are three things you want to get out of this position?
34. What do you plan to do outside of the workplace to succeed in this job?
35. In what ways do you foresee developing yourself professionally in this position?
36. In what ways do you foresee developing yourself personally in this position?

Teamwork Questions

Here's another big category for interviewers. They want to know how well you work and play with others.

37. What types of co-workers do you work well with?
38. What types of co-workers do you not work well with?
39. In a team environment, what role do you typically play?
40. What three strengths do you bring to a team, especially as they relate to this job?

41. What is a more natural role for you in a team?
    A. Team leader
    B. Peacemaker
    C. Task manager
    D. Follower
42. On a team, in which role do you feel most comfortable?
    A. Take-charge person
    B. Facilitator
    C. Supporter
43. Tell me about a time you had to rally your team to complete a project.
44. Tell about a time when a teammate did not carry his/her weight.
45. What would you do if you noticed a colleague struggling at work?
46. Tell me about a time when you were part of a group and your project or task went differently than what you wanted or expected?
47. Describe a situation where you successfully worked in a team and a situation where you struggled with it.
48. Tell me about a time you were leading a team on a new initiative. How did you approach it?
49. What role did you play on the team in Question 48?
50. How do you handle team members who are critical of your performance?
51. Tell me about a time when you were part of a toxic team.
52. How did you handle the situation as a leader or as a member of a toxic team?

Leadership Questions

Interviewers will get around to this critical category. They always have their eyes peeled for the next leader in the organization.

53. What are the top three leadership strengths you possess?
54. How have you demonstrated your top three leadership strengths?
55. What is one weakness or blind spot of your leadership style?
56. How have you tried to overcome a weakness in your leadership style?
57. Of those in current leadership positions or roles (in or outside of our industry), whom do you admire the most and why?

58. Of the leadership roles you've held, which one taught you the most and why?
59. How do you establish trust, credibility, and respect in a leadership role?
60. What are the biggest challenges you have faced in your leadership role?
61. What is your leadership style?
62. How do you engage your team?
63. Tell me a time when you were frustrated with an authority figure.
64. What steps did you take to improve the working relationship with an authority figure?
65. As a leader, what would you do if your leadership style was ineffective?
66. Tell me about a time when you were on a team that lacked leadership.
67. How did you deal with being on a team that lacked leadership?
68. In hindsight, is there anything you would have changed or done differently?
69. How would you characterize your leadership style?
70. What strategies do you use to inspire and motivate your team or co-workers?
71. Tell me about a time when, in order to do your job, you had to establish credibility and respect as a leader.
72. If you were trying to find a successor, what three attributes would you want to cultivate in that person, and why?
73. As you reflect back on your development as a leader, what is your leadership style?
74. How has your leadership style evolved?
75. Give me an example of how you have been an innovative leader in your current or most recent position.

Communication/Self-Management Questions

These questions examine your preferred communication style and how you manage yourself. Interviewers will assess your communication skills during the interview, as well as how you communicate with your co-workers. If you do not communicate well, the interview will be a very short and tough process.

76. How do you determine the best communication style to use when working with different co-workers?

77. Your boss just gave you an important project that is due tomorrow. How do you enlist your team to help?

78. What form of communication are you most comfortable with and why? .

79. What are you doing to develop the areas that need improvement?

80. If you are new in a job and cannot handle your growing list of tasks and responsibilities, what do you do?
    A. Stay later.
    B. Work smarter.
    C. Ask for help.

81. What are your hot buttons?

82. What situations bring out your hot buttons?

83. How do you handle it when your hot buttons are pushed?

84. Tell me about an area you've decided to work on in your life.

85. What one area would you most like to improve, and how do you plan to address it?

86. Tell me about a time when you received constructive feedback and how you responded?

87. What three unique qualities do you bring to this position?

Self-Awareness Questions

These questions focus on your self-perception and objectivity.

88. How do you see yourself?

89. Looking back to your childhood, what one positive experience has shaped you the most?

90. When do others look to you for advice, and when do they look elsewhere?

91. Tell me about a time when you did not achieve your goal and what you learned from that experience.

92. What would keep you from staying in this position after you started?

93. Tell me about a time you weren't able to finish something you had started. What did you feel and how did you cope with this feeling?

94. How do you feel when someone on your team doesn't fulfill his/her commitment?

95. Looking back over the course of your life to date, what has been the most valuable constructive criticism you have received?
96. What is a common misconception people have about you?
97. Tell me about a critical team disagreement and your role in the disagreement.

Skill-Based Questions

These questions apply to the specific job requirements of the position and require very straightforward answers.

98. Tell me about your experiences working with Linux systems, Ubuntu, and other open source systems.
99. How would you rate your performance on working with Outlook, Excel, and PowerPoint®?
100. What is the largest number of workers you have supervised?
101. How familiar are you with our accounting software, and how much experience have you had?
102. How many sales jobs have you had?

Offbeat Questions

These off-the-wall interview questions might catch you off guard, but they are designed to add levity to the interview, assess your creativity, and demonstrate how quickly you can think on your feet. Do your best in answering them, and try to have a little fun if you can. We heard these intriguing questions recently.

103. If you were an animal, what kind of animal would you be?
104. If you were an insect, what would you be?
105. If an alien visited Earth, what kind of music would they listen to?
106. What were your PSAT, ACT, or SAT scores? Do they accurately reflect your abilities?
107. Tell me about the best boss you ever had.
108. Tell me about the worst boss you ever had.
109. What is the temperature when it is twice as cold as zero degrees?

110. Describe yourself in three words.
111. On a scale of 1 to 10, with 10 being the highest, how happy are you?
112. What would increase your happiness, outside of getting this job?
113. How would you design a spice rack for a blind person?
114. What were the top three causes of the Civil War?
115. What are the first three things you would do on your first day at work here?
116. Do you like Tom or Jerry? Veronica or Betty? Elmer or Bugs? Superwoman or Batwoman? Paper or plastic?
117. What video or online games do you play on a regular basis?
118. If you could visit an ancient place, which one would you like to visit?
119. If you had a time machine, what place and point in time would you go?
120. If you were a super hero, who would you be, and what would your special power be?
121. How would you react if you were transformed into a fish? A bear? A mosquito?
122. What famous person would you like to meet, and why?
123. What does your refrigerator say about you?
124. If I looked inside your refrigerator, what would I find?
125. Tell me about a recent travel experience.
126. If you had to guess, how many licks would it take to get to the middle of a Tootsie pop? How did you come up with that number?
127. If you could speak to an animal, what animal would it be, and what would you say to it?
128. What is your preferred attire when you are working?
129. If I gave you $1 million, what would you do with it?
130. How would $1 million change your life?
131. What was your most embarrassing situation in the last 10 years?
132. How many hats do you have? What's your favorite?
133. If you were a T-shirt, what would be printed on you?
134. How do they get deer to cross at those yellow signs?
135. What was the greatest thing before sliced bread?
136. What was the greatest thing after sliced bread?
137. If working here were like being on LSD, how would you describe it?
138. Tell me a joke.
139. Which magical power would you pick and why—flying, invisibility, or teleportation?

140. What would be the title of your autobiography?
141. What words would be carved on your headstone?
142. What three fictional characters would you invite to a dinner party?
143. If you were stranded on a desert island, which three books would you want to read?

Closing Comments and Questions

When the interviewer asks if you have any additional comments or questions, it indicates that your meeting has come to an end. Always speak up—even if you are just highlighting your qualifications or summarizing key points in the interview.

144. "I'm finished with all of my questions. Do you have any questions that come to mind about this position? If not, then the next steps in the process will be to take this information to the review committee, and we will have a decision within two weeks."
145. "Thank you for coming in today. It has been a pleasure meeting you, and it was interesting getting to know you. In the next few minutes, is there anything else you want to share that will help us in our selection process?"
146. "I enjoyed getting to know you. Is there anything you would like to ask me about the position or our organization? Thank you for coming by, we will get in touch with you soon."
147. "I've asked all of the necessary questions to help me determine if there's a fit. Do you feel comfortable that you have shared everything that you wanted with us? Is there anything you want to add?"
148. "Do you feel comfortable that you have told us everything you wanted? Is there anything else that you would like to share with the panel that hasn't already been discussed?"
149. "Is there anything else you would like to share with us that we have not had a chance to talk about? The next steps in the application process will be presenting this information to the selection committee, and you'll be hearing from us in the next few weeks."
150. "Our time has ended, and I need to wrap things up. Thank you for coming in to interview today. I have thoroughly enjoyed getting to know you. I hope to see you in this new job. You did a great job, and this was a crazy good interview."

Illegal Questions

Various federal, state, and local laws regulate the questions a prospective employer can ask job applicants. It is illegal to ask questions related to your age, sex, race, religion, national origin, or marital status, or to delve into your personal life for information that is not job-related. An employer's questions on a job application, in the interview, or during the hiring process must be related to the job being applied for. The employer must focus on: "What do I need to know to determine that this candidate can perform the job functions?"

If asked an illegal question, you can respond in three ways:

1. You can answer the question, but you are divulging information that is not related to the job.
2. You can ask the interviewer to explain how the question relates to the job. If you do not see the connection, then you can politely refuse to answer. In this case, you run the risk of appearing uncooperative.
3. You can respond with an answer as it might apply to the job. If the interviewer asks an illegal question, such as, "Are you a U.S. citizen?" you can say that you are authorized to work in the United States.

Nationality

Legal: Are you authorized to work in the United States?
What languages do you read, speak, or write fluently? (This question is acceptable if it relates to performing the job.)
Illegal: Were you born in the United States?
Where were your parents born?
What is your native language?

Age

Legal: Are you over 18?
Illegal: How old are you?
When were you born?

Personal Information

Illegal: How tall are you?
How much do you weigh?

Marital/Family Status

Legal: Are you willing to relocate?
Are you willing to travel as part of the job?
Can you work overtime, if required?
Illegal: Are you married?
Are you divorced?
Do you have small children?
Who takes care of them?

Disabilities

Legal: Can you perform the essential functions of this job with or without reasonable accommodations? (This question is acceptable if the interviewer thoroughly described the job.)
Illegal: Do you have any disabilities?
Have you had any recent or past illnesses or operations?
Do you have any chronic medical problems?
When was your last physical exam?
Are your family members healthy?

Affiliations

Legal: Do you belong to any professional organizations that are relevant to your ability to perform this job?
Illegal: To what clubs or social organizations do you belong?

Arrest Record

Legal: Have you ever been convicted of _____? (The crime must relate to the performance of the job in question.)
Illegal: Were you ever arrested?
Have you served time in the big house?

Military

Legal: What type of training or education did you receive in the military?
Illegal: In what military branch did you serve?
Were you honorably discharged?

Discrimination

If you believe an employer did not hire you for a job because of your age, color, sex, religion, national origin, marital status, or disability, you can file a claim with the U.S. Equal Employment Opportunity Commission (EEOC) at www.eeoc.gov/facts/howtofil.html.

Questions to Ask Interviewers

At the End of the Pre-Screening Interview

1. "I have reviewed the job description and perused your website. Are there any other traits (or experiences) you are looking for (or you are interested in) that I might address with you?"
2. "Is there any additional information I can provide to help you in this screening process?"
3. "When do you plan on selecting an individual for this position?"
4. "Is there any additional information I should read to get a deeper understanding of this position or the organization?"

At the End of a Selection Interview

1. "If you had to rank the different aspects (or requirements) of this position, what would be your top three in terms of importance? Is there one aspect that is more heavily weighted than the other two?"
2. "What does a successful employee look like in this corporation? If you could clone the most successful employee you have, what would this clone look like?"
3. "What characteristics are most valued by this organization? Why do think so?"
4. "For you, what are the top three things that you believe this organization does better than its competition? Than anyone else?"
5. "If you could change one thing about this position, what would it be and why?"

6. "If you could change one thing about this corporation, what would it be and why?"
7. "What has been your career path to your current position?"
8. "What is the organization's top strategic objective? Do you see it changing in the coming year?"
9. "What are the greatest external threats to this organization? How is this organization handling those threats?"

Index